GENERATION EXILE
THE LIVES I LEAVE BEHIND

A Memoir by Rodrigo Dorfman

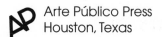

Arte Público Press
Houston, Texas

Generation Exile: The Lives I Leave Behind is published in part with support from the National Endowment for the Arts. We are grateful for its support.

Recovering the past, creating the future

Arte Público Press
University of Houston
4902 Gulf Fwy, Bldg 19, Rm 100
Houston, Texas 77204-2004

Cover design by Mora Designs

Names: Dorfman, Rodrigo, author.
Title: Generation exile : the lives I leave behind / a memoir by Rodrigo Dorfman.
Other titles: Lives I leave behind
Description: Houston, Texas : Arte Público Press, [2023] | Summary: "If you ever sing those songs again, they will kill your daddy," the boy's mother warned him after he continued to sing one of the hymns of the Chilean revolution in public. Rodrigo Dorfman, the son of prominent dissidents, was six years old when his family fled Augusto Pinochet's military dictatorship a month after the CIA-backed coup in 1973. In his fascinating memoir, Dorfman writes about his experiences as an exile and a migrant. He was dragged away from his homeland, "seduced by the thrill of flying on airplanes and visiting far-away places," but reassured the family would return soon. They fled to Argentina, and then to Havana, Paris, Amsterdam and finally Bethesda, Maryland. His muse and identity were "sealed and stamped with that curse, with that blessing, with that irresistible myth: the eternal return." Mapping the memory of exile, he remembers the contradiction of living with his seething anger at losing his home and his resistance to settling down. Rebellion was an ancestral badge of honor he wore proudly. At 18, he returned to Chile and fought against the fascist dictatorship, running for his life with bullets and tear gas flying by. Dorfman's involvement in the resistance movement there planted the seeds for his future life as a community-centered documentary filmmaker. His restless search for a place to call his own led to his wandering-around the United States, to Morocco and Turkey and the Path of Sufism. He finally made a home in the American South, where he became a "Latino" and found kinship with other immigrants who settled there. This compelling narrative recounts a displaced man's life-long quest to establish family, roots and a sense of belonging by bearing witness to what he calls the "Nuevo South." RODRIGO DORFMAN is a Chilean-born, Latino award-winning writer and filmmaker. His documentaries have been screened at festivals around the world. His feature, FIESTA! Quinceañera on the intersection of quinceañeras and immigrant traditions in the South, and his feature documentary, Quaranteened, were broadcast on PBS stations. His photographs have been exhibited at museums across the United States. He is an associate member of La Pocha Nostra and a community activist in his adopted hometown of (HE LIVES IN) Durham, North Carolina, where he lives with his wife Primm and their children"— Provided by publisher.
Identifiers: LCCN 2022060522 (print) | LCCN 2022060523 (ebook) |
    ISBN 9781558859623 (paperback) | ISBN 9781518507540 (epub) |
    ISBN 9781518507557 (kindle edition) | ISBN 9781518507564 (pdf)
Subjects: LCSH: Dorfman, Rodrigo. | Chilean Americans—North Carolina—Durham—Biography. |
    Exiles—Chile—Santiago—Biography. | Exiles—United States—Biography. | Chile—Politics and
    government—1973-1988. | Motion picture producers and directors—North Carolina—Durham—
    Biography. | Durham (N.C.)—Biography. | Santiago (Chile)—Biography.
Classification: LCC F264.D8 D67 2023 (print) | LCC F264.D8 (ebook) |
DDC 973/.046883092 [B]—dc23/eng/20221228
LC record available at https://lccn.loc.gov/2022060522
LC ebook record available at https://lccn.loc.gov/2022060523

♾ The paper used in this publication meets the requirements of the American National Standard for Information Sciences—Permanence of Paper for Printed Library Materials, ANSI Z39.48-1984.

My story is not a pleasant one; it is neither sweet nor harmonious, as invented stories are; it has the taste of nonsense and chaos, of madness and dreams—like the lives of all men who stop deceiving themselves.

Herman Hesse

CONTENTS

BOOK IV: Songs for a New Home

INTRODUCTION
The Art of Loss

Ever since I left Chile as a child, I've been looking for a home, a piece of earth, a peace of mind, a place where my lives can rest for a while beneath the shade of a tree I have planted, a garden I have tended, under the roof of a house I can call my own. My journey has been a labyrinth of identities, a cosmic hall of broken mirrors reflecting all the lives, latitudes and multitudes I have whirled with during the first fifty years of my life.

As I look back, I see myself and my generation coming of age suspended between centuries and millennia, in a world marked by the catastrophe of the Reagan years and the inevitable fall of the Berlin Wall. I see the first generation in US history to experience the death of the American Dream and the aggravated childhood trauma of divorce and separation.

We are Generation Exile.

The X in our name marks the spot where the treasure lies; the X is the anonymous rebel, the crossroad and the riddle of the Sphinx, a phonetic chameleon and ancient symbol of transformation; the X-ray, the great multiplier, the mystery in any equation.

We got lost for what feels like a very long time.

And yet, what I've discovered in my travels and zigzags is that the experience of exile and migration has that rare quality that can illuminate some of the most intimate choices we make on the path of becoming who we are. We are reborn, it seems, at the crossroads. We choose a life, and we leave one behind. What better way to travel into the unknown than to embody the power of the metaphor to shape not just our consciousness but also the physical world around us?

I remember my last day in Amsterdam, standing on one of those crossroads, the one that cuts like a knife between childhood and adolescence. It was the summer of 1981, I was fourteen, still young and wild, barely aware of myself. I was speaking French at school and street Dutch with my neighborhood friends. I had learned English watching *Benny Hill* and *I, Claudius* on the BBC and spoke Spanish, my mother tongue at home. Our small Dutch apartment was now empty; everything of value amassed during those past four sedentary years was packed away in numbered cardboard boxes ready to be shipped (along with us) on a cargo boat across the Atlantic toward our new home in the USA. The bulk of the boxes consisted of my father's improbably large library of books and writings he had accumulated since going into our exile from Chile under Augusto Pinochet's dictatorship. I was six years old then, barely hanging on to my stuffed rabbit as we made our escape one month after the CIA-backed military coup of September 11, 1973, that destroyed the democratically elected government of Salvador Allende and much of my childhood innocence along with it. My mother and I escaped first with just a couple of suitcases. My father stayed behind, hiding from the military death squads in the relative safety and sanctuary of the besieged Argentinian embassy in Santiago with only the clothes on his back and a donated blanket for comfort. The rest of our belongings remained behind in our house in Santiago a house we hoped the fascists wouldn't ransack and pillage during those first savage months of the military coup that claimed thousands of lives and forced one tenth of the Chilean population to flee in a mass exodus into the uncertain waters of political exile . . . like we did.

Like any good wandering Jew, my father loved his books. They were part of his identity as a writer and a lover of stories. Knowing that they were coming along with us across the waters must have offered him a glimmer of belonging in the midst of loss, just like my mother who loved to hang on to every bit of clothing she ever bought during those long days of our early exile. For me, back then in Amsterdam, those past four years had been the longest stretch of time I had ever lived anywhere in one place on this Earth. Still, I played along. I was ready to leave my childhood behind, and so I sold or gave away my bigger toys and my large collection of kids' books. But there was one bulky item I did not want to part with: a tall cylindrical laundry box filled with thousands of porcelain, glass and metal marbles. I had started collecting them when I landed in my first French school back in 1974, in Palaiseau, a small town on the outskirts of Paris. I had won many of those marbles during countless games of chance and dexterity. They were my treasure, the one palpable constant in my short life. Deep down, I must have known that they offered a sense of belonging in the same way that books were a refuge during my father's restless wanderings. Of course, back then, if I had been conscious of this powerful metaphor, all I would have had to do was look my father in the eyes and tell him that every single memory of my exile was contained within each one of those marbles. Tears would have flowed. He would have melted away with that pained look I have seen burdening him so many countless times. I know that he and my mother would have done anything to get those marbles on that ship. But I didn't. Back then, I didn't live in a world of metaphors the way I do today. Back then, I roamed the world armed only with my savage instinct for survival.

So instead, I took charge of my destiny. I carried the child-hood object of my desire to our small brick terrace on the third floor of our apartment building. I took a peek at our perfectly trimmed and paved Dutch neighborhood built from the ashes of WWII. The coast was clear. With all the might of my pounding little heart, I lifted the box and dropped all the marbles over the parapet into the clean and spotless symmetrical street.

A thousand jewels thrown to the winds.

I stood there, holding my breath, marveling that it would take years for all the kids in the neighborhood to find those hidden treasures of my exile . . . one shiny marbled memory after another.

I told this story, some thirty years later, to my two daughters. Isabella was ten and Catalina seven, both born in Durham, North Carolina. We were sitting around the kitchen table, dinner was over. My wife at the time was away on a research trip and we were talking about loss, a theme probably brought on by the sudden death of Catalina's classroom guinea pig the day before.

"I didn't have to throw those marbles out the window, did I?" I asked after they'd heard the story.

They shook their heads.

"That's right. But you see, if I was going to lose them anyway, well, I wanted to make sure I would never ever forget *how* I lost them. So, I did the most dramatic thing I could imagine. I threw them out the window."

They smiled. I have no idea what they were thinking.

"So, here's my question," I continued. "If you had to choose between having those marbles in the attic in a box somewhere or having a glorious story about how you left them behind, what would you choose? Take your time."

I stood up to get their chocolate ice cream out of the freezer. I paused, letting the cold breeze against my face take my mind, as it often does, to another place. A movie theatre. I had recently seen the film adaptation of Cormac McCarthy's book *The Road*, about a father who travels with his young son across a post-apocalyptic landscape in search of salvation. There was something, something I wondered, about Viggo Mortensen's heart-breaking performance that reminded me of this seemingly innocent question I had asked my children. Of course, the circumstances were different. I was in my bright, middle-class kitchen, scooping ice cream for my daughters, while he was in that frigid nuclear winter confronted with the total breakdown of society, desperately trying to hang on to that fire, to that love, to that mystery that makes us human. I saw the film one winter afternoon with my father in a movie theatre whose heating system had absurdly decided to stop working. As we huddled against each other in the cold and witnessed *The Road* take us down that dark and ambiguous place of what it means to be a survivor, I couldn't help thinking about my daughters. Just like that desperate father, I wondered what words, what stories and metaphors I would give my children to describe the world we live in. How do you prepare them for that dawn that comes when you'll have to leave them behind and trust that you've poured every single drop of your humanity into them?

I don't remember what my daughters answered that night. But as I write these words, I know that my life was shaped by my choice to leave those childhood marbles behind, just like it was shaped by the many fateful choices I made during my long wandering years. They're the kind of choices that come after you take that primordial fall down a well and the darkness descends upon you and you have to make sense of the loss of a loved one, of a country or a home. And if you're patient and you allow the darkness to envelop you, to bury you in its mysterious loving shroud, if you can experience all the pain and all the joy that comes from swimming in that darkness, if you can withstand that savage, sweet burning, then your eyes will slowly begin to adjust and you'll begin to see.

This is where our journey begins. As we travel through the pages of this book—this pound of my flesh—and into the black ink from which these words are born, ask yourself: What gift will you carry with you as you emerge from the darkness into the light?

BOOK I

SONGS OF EXILE

AND I ALWAYS THOUGHT
And I always thought: the very simplest words
Must be enough. When I say what things are like
Everyone's heart must be torn to shreds.
That you'll go down if you don't stand up for yourself
Surely you see that.

Bertolt Brecht

IN THE GARDEN OF
SOCIALIST DELIGHTS
(Chile, 1973)

I live in a world shaped by the senses, where I can still frolic naked in the rain in a constant state of blooming euphoria, and the wind in my hair is just that, a pure sensation, nothing more, nothing less. A soft tickle, a caress, an invisible kiss from a faraway star in the night. I am pre-abstract, even pre-historic. Wild, savage and free. In other words: joyfully illiterate and unstoppable. I'm sure there's a clinical description for this condition. When you're six, they call it hyperactive, and when it's a whole country, they call it a revolution. At least that's how I imagine myself in 1973, during those last glorious months of the Chilean Revolution before the military coup, before exile, before the Pinochets of this world entered my life and poisoned the well of my childhood paradise.

Never in history had a country decided, by democratic means, to peacefully attempt to dismantle its capitalist system and give millions of its peasants and working-class citizens the dignity and the power to finally be masters of their own destinies. It would be as if the United States Congress and President Joe Biden, after the 2020 elections, had ended corporate welfare as we know it, nationalized the energy sector, created universal health care, raised the minimum wage to an actual living wage and financed the creation of large public works that benefitted the 99%. That's just for starters. Of course, history doesn't just happen, no matter how much our present global consumer culture of amnesia seduces us into believing that Facebook, Twitter and the Kardashians are central engines of historical processes. No, the historical Chilean elections of 1970 that brought to power a leftist coalition of political parties was the product of more than fifty years of revolutionary consciousness transmitted from generation to generation, with one of the highest literacy rates in the continent, and from uprising to uprising, in what was a bloody twentieth century.

Reflecting on the power of the Chilean Revolution during an interview for my documentary "Occupy the Imagination," my father told me, "Listen, Rodrigo, reality is up for grabs. I know it's difficult to think that this is possible. We can define reality any way we want. This was only possible because the whole of a country, the whole of a continent, the whole world was moving in the direction of saying, 'We can change everything.' You don't have to leave the world as it was when you were born. 'Yes, we can,' we said back then. And we said another world is possible. Another world is possible, right now!"

The whole of Chile seemed like an extension of my school playground. While adults worked to change the world, children played dangerous games of class warfare at recess, like factory takeovers, with the capitalist pigs holed up in an empty cracked swimming pool in the middle of our school yard while we fought, throwing sticks and stones at each other—literally. Nobody lost an eye, but I dreamt it once: an arrow shot straight into my eye. It must have been after I got into a political argument with the neighbor boy two houses down the street. I think I called him "a right-wing son of a bitch." The sad truth of those days of black and white, when everyone was at each other's throats, is that cursing became an essential tool of political expression. Sure, there are the harmless and absurd ones that rhymed like "*¡Blanco! ¡Amarillo! ¡Momio sin calzoncillos!*" (White! Yellow! Right-winger without underwear!), but more common was, "*¡Date una vuelta en el aire, momio concha de tu madre!*" (Why don't you do a summersault, right-wing motherfucker!). It was bad, all right, and unfortunately, my neighbor, who was no more than a year older than me, hit me with a large branch right in the face, barely missing my eye. A taste of things to come? Before I knew it, I was bleeding and crying, and my mother was standing in front of their house shouting at the top of her lungs, "Shit's going to happen," or something like that.

Like so many of my generation, I was born into revolution. My father was named Vladimiro for Lenin and so, in turn, my parents made sure my middle name was Fidel, after Cuba's Castro. And then there's the classic poster of Karl Marx, the one with the giant gray beard, hanging on the wall above my father's messy desk. We called him Papá Marx, sort of a Santa Claus figure without his magical reindeers or the elves with their pointy ears. I can't exactly remember what Papá Marx did, but as good assimilated Jews, we celebrated Christmas with a big ham garnished with slices of roasted pineapple.

I confess: I did not know I was Jewish until my first month in exile, when some kids in Argentina called me "a dirty Jew." But I digress. At age six, I could happily argue the non-existence of God because I was a proud fourth-generation atheist, and I knew all the greatest hits:

"If there's a God, why are there poor children who go to bed hungry?"

"And if there's a God and he lets children starve, then he's a bad God."

And my favorite: "Who needs God, anyway?"

I knew I was not just merely parroting my father trying to convert his best friends to atheism, because you cannot fake the power of your convictions. It was the early seventies, and the world was black and white. We were the good guys, and the fascists with their flags embroidered with white crosses were the bad guys. How can anyone argue with that? It's like telling Jesus to get off the cross, asking the Soviets not to charge the Winter

Palace or trying to convince Rosa Parks to sit at the back of the bus. You can't.

My childhood drawings reflected this idealistic utopia. First, the customary triangular Andes mountains in the background with their eternal snow peaks and a bright yellow sun, smiling. Below, stick figures of factory workers in their yellow hard hats, raised fists, like little balls (because I didn't know how to draw fingers), hand in hand with students and peasants, their big straw hats and chickens everywhere. Learning how to read and write was fun. Drawing chickens was even better. My school was the experimental Colegio Latinoamericano de Integración, better known as *el Latino*, located at the time on Pedro de Valdivia Avenue in the heart of the fading aristocratic neighborhood of Providencia, with its magnificent tree-lined boulevards and a mix of ornate *fin-de-siècle* French-styled mansions, *petit bourgeois* apartments and upper middle-class stucco houses with their gardeners and maids reminding us that Chile had always been in the hands of the ruling class—and no dirty hippie commie was going to take that away from them. Of course, in Chile, nothing is as it ever seems. As a teenager, my father grew up not far from my school in one of those two-story houses with a maid and a cook. His parents had immigrated from the United States in 1954, after my grandfather Adolfo, who worked at the United Nations, was denounced as an agent of the great communist conspiracy by none other than Senator Joseph McCarthy, in the flesh. He told the Secretary General of the United Nations to "get that troublemaker Adolfo Dorfman out of here, or else." The next thing you know, my grandfather Adolfo is re-assigned to Santiago, Chile, to work on the post-war industrialization of Latin America. And my father, in a figment of my imagination, is dragged away, kicking and screaming from his life as a hot-dog-eating, comic-book-collecting, Yankees fan, Howdy Doody all-American boy and forced into his new Chilean existence, where at some point he's lucky enough to meet my mother at a screening of Disney's *Pollyanna*. And, lo and behold, there I was, six years old, sitting in a classroom full of children singing revolutionary anthems, joyfully dancing down the yellow brick road of democratic socialism, all the while oblivious to the irony that I am the historical (or was it coincidental?) creation of the sick and twisted mind of one Joseph McCarthy.

I would like to imagine that the malevolent ghost of Joe Mc-Carthy was not haunting my story back then, that paradise was truly paradise, pure and unblemished in my mind, without a single tinge of regret. I mean, what six-year-old has regrets? "I should have known" is one of those beginnings that seem to lead nowhere, like an Escher staircase. There's a mystery in those empty steps that mirrors the process of remembering, like the strip of negative space between the flickering frames of a projected movie reel creating the illusion of continuous motion in the intimate darkness of a theatre where I sit and see myself on a field trip to a brand-new, luminous poultry hatchery on the outskirts of Santiago. It's mesmerizing. The eggs, the incubators, the thousands of puffy yellow chicks with their tiny beaks, squeaking, chirping at the world as they roll past us on those endless moving conveyer belts.

And all we wanted to do was to take a chick home, our excited glances told each other. And that's exactly what happened. The next thing, as in a dream, I had two little chicks curled up in the deep pockets of my school apron. They were warm and fuzzy, and I did my best to ignore the look on my mother's face when I stretched out my hands and showed them to her later that afternoon. What the heck were the teachers thinking? And what to do with them? Raise them in your city backyard? In your apartment complex? In the middle of a revolution? My mother put them in an old shoe box, and we mixed white cotton and grass leaves and some dirt and kept them in there at night. During the day, we let them run around the yard. They were safe because my parents had built a tall stucco wall around the house after a group of right-wingers specifically targeted our home, throwing stones and trash because my father, along with Armand Mattelart, a Belgian sociologist, had recently published a book called *How to Read Donald Duck*, a fearless and humorous Marxist analysis of imperialist cultural ideology in the Disney comics exported to Latin America in the 60s and 70s. It was a book that would change my life. But, I'm getting ahead of myself, because before bringing to the surface the burning of books, I need to account for the tragic death of those two innocent chicks.

Pato, my best friend, was visiting and we were playing with the water hose. Chasing, splashing, frolicking in the muddy grass. It's easy to lose yourself when you're having so much fun and there is so little parental control. It was the seventies, after all, and in our intoxication we decided to give those stinky chicks a shower. We let them loose and chased them around the yard with the water hose and our squeaks of laughter. We terrorized them. There's no other way to describe it.

That night, they started shivering with an upper respiratory infection. We tried to warm them up under a hot lamp, but nothing really helped. There I was, standing over the shoe box with that glaring light exposing every wheezing sound, every tremor and spasm of their fragile little bodies, for what seemed like hours, silently punishing myself for what I had done. I had never seen death before. I was fascinated and horrified at the same time.

I'm too young to fantasize or even conjure up Henry Kissinger, the architect of the military coup and Nixon's national security advisor at the time, looking down on this sad episode, shaking his head, saying with a Peter Sellers, Dr. Strangelove accent, "I don't see why we need to stand by and watch a country go communist due to the irresponsibility of its own people." Of course, the reason Kissinger's hair was on fire was not the death of my innocent chicks; the real, real reason was that since 1958, the CIA had spent more than six million dollars directly intervening in Chile's electoral processes in an effort to make sure that Salvador Allende, or anyone like him, would never get elected. From creating fake news stories, having journalists on their payroll, subsidizing political parties and terrorism, producing radio spots and propaganda posters featuring hungry communists literally eating babies, the CIA wrote the book that Putin happily updated in 2016 to intervene in the US presidential elections. Kissinger's rhetorical question posed before the Forty Committee, a secret group in charge of greenlighting all covert "black" operations against any foreign government slipping out of the US orbit of influence, made it clear that they were ready to "make the Chilean economy scream." As Edward Korry, then US ambassador to Chile, described it, ". . . to do all within our power to condemn Chile and the Chileans to utmost deprivation and poverty." In other words, economic chaos.

By mid-June 1973, one gray winter morning, I was standing near the Canal San Carlos, a few blocks from the little bungalow that was our home on Vaticano Street, holding my father's hand as we waited for the public bus to take me to school. The ground was wet, and a cold drizzle chilled our bones and filled the air with a sense of dread and doom. I was late for school, and even smoking an invisible cigarette with the steam puffing from my breath was no longer fun. My father looked worried, angry, frustrated.

Today, I can imagine the weight that he was carrying. The country was in chaos and the CIA's campaign to destabilize Chile in full swing: fascist paramilitary organizations were bombing bridges, electric power pylons, water viaducts and railroads; shortages of basic staples like flour and sugar became rampant; a trucker strike almost paralyzed the country; radical left-wing groups taking advantage of the situation were illegally occupying land and seizing factories; and the tightening of the US economic and financial embargo was devastating the economy. One third of all private and public buses were completely inoperative due to the lack of spare parts and tires because manufacturers such as Ford had stopped selling them to Chile. And that, in a nutshell, is my epic excuse as to why I was late for school. It didn't make the cold any warmer or the waiting any shorter, and little did I know that this was probably the last time I would stand on that corner with my father waiting for a bus that would never come.

Soon, everything was going to change. Rapidly.

On June 29th, a rogue tank division took to the streets of Santiago in a seemingly improvised military coup. Shots were fired; there was hesitation from certain factions of the Army, but at the end of the day, the civilian conspirators fled into the Ecuadorian embassy and a certain General Augusto Pinochet, undistinguished until then, demonstrated a particular zest in putting the rebellion down. Pinochet, of course, was secretly preparing to lead the successful military coup a few months later, proving that this episode was nothing more than a setup to test how the population would react and, more importantly, to find out who was truly loyal to the government of President Salvador Allende. Many of those loyalists would be the first ones to be shot in the early hours of September 11, 1973.

After the failed coup in June, we moved out of our bungalow for security reasons and went to live with my grandparents in the heart of Providencia, surrounded by many of the very people who would soon cheer and welcome, with the popping sound of champagne bottles, the destruction of my paradise.

I would never see my childhood home again.

THE FALL
(Chile, 1973)

The sky was bright blue, the air crystal clear. There was a calm pierced only by the sounds of Hawker Hunter jets flying over Santiago on their way to bomb the presidential palace, where my father should have been working that day, and by his account should have also died alongside his *compañeros* and the president he swore to defend.

But he didn't. Fate had other plans for him.

As for me, in my six-year-old mind, there was only a blurred sense of days feeding one into the other in a dreamlike darkness. No blue skies, no scintillating snowcapped Andes holding Santiago in their indifferent embrace. No close-up of my innocent eyes looking up at the heavens and pointing my little index finger at the low-flying jets in a perfectly framed Spielberg moment. No. Just the night, the drawn, thick curtains and the dimmed lights of my grandparents' mid-century living room. I see myself standing on the landing of the wide wooden staircase leading to the second floor, hiding behind one of the pillars of the balustrade, watching my mother and my grandparents below listening to a singular voice on the radio. It's threatening, nasal, invading. It's the voice of General Augusto Pinochet, Commander in Chief of the Armed Forces and now president of the military junta, declaring in no uncertain terms, as I will learn years later, the imposition of a state of siege across the country and the indefinite suspension of the Chilean constitution.

This was the end of fifty years of continuous constitutional rule, the longest such period in Latin American history. I didn't need to know those historical facts to realize that something terrible had just happened. I could read it on my mother's face. I could see it in the glaring absence of my father. I was an anxious child, and the recurring paralyzing knot in my stomach made it hard to breathe. I could feel a creeping sensation of guilt slowly washing over me during those early days before we would flee the country into exile. It is hard to imagine that barely a week ago I was still in school, playing with my friends and neighbors in my personal paradise. I'm sure my parents, like so many others, did not want to burden their children with the impending sense of doom of the inevitable coup that everyone knew was coming.

There was no escape. A week before the coup, outside the gates of my school, the fury of the right-wing populace had reached fever pitch. We called them *momios,* "the mummies," because of their antiquated, decrepit political values and affected bourgeois mannerisms, patronizing stares, excessive make-up. They were wrapped in furs and expensive coats as they marched down the streets, banging their empty pots symbolizing the lack of staples, such as sugar and flour, in local stores. How we hated them. I remember, forty-three years later, in 2016, standing at a Trump rally in Johnston County, North Carolina, watching, in disbelief: the same hairdos, the same fake eyelashes and powdered faces, the same fear and hatred in their eyes disguised as flag-waving righteous patriotism. There are so many ways we can be emotionally triggered by the past. . . . Sometimes all it takes is a crooked smile, and I get thrown back to that day, one week before the coup, when the *momios* marched in front of our school, taunting us with their desire to destroy us.

I'm not sure how it happened. Maybe it was during recess? Or the teachers, already on the edge of the precipice, just let us out without a leash?

We rushed like wild horses toward the metal gates of the school and started throwing rocks at the pot-banging crowd. Big ones, small ones, anything our little hands could grab. The teachers tried to stop us, but it was too late. The enraged *momios* charged the gate, and the teachers blocked them with their bodies. The riot police jumped in, there was tear gas and a fight and maybe even water cannons? My hands gripped the cold iron pickets of the fence, my face barely squeezed between them as I watched the chaos. I knew that we had done something very bad. Maybe if it weren't for the dead chicks I killed, I wouldn't have developed such a heightened sense of guilt, forever now entangled with that haunting voice of Pinochet coming at me from the small radio in the middle of the night. It was a voice I could feel snaking inside of me, attaching itself like a parasite into the very fiber of that traumatic experience. Of course, I thought that my father was dead and that I was to blame and that I should lose myself in every possible worst-case scenario my distorted six-year-old imagination was creating for me. I still find it hard to believe that as a six-year-old I lived with that secret anguish even for a day, but then again, one of the reasons we pick at our scabs is to remind ourselves that we belong in a time of pain and sorrow.

At that moment, I did not know my father was on the run from safe house to safe house, stubbornly refusing to leave Chile for exile, the military noose slowly tightening around him. My mother was left to deal with the little details that mark the difference between life and death. Two days later, after the daytime curfew was lifted, she returned to our old home, which by some miracle had not yet been stormed and ransacked by the military, and began to destroy every single incriminating poster, flyer, pamphlet and piece of paper she could find. It was an unseasonably warm end of winter, and a dead give-away of our guilt was the plume of black smoke rising above our house, carrying with it bits and pieces of our revolutionary past now literally turned to ashes before our eyes. Not wanting to take any chances, my mother dumped every piece of paper in a bassinet back in the laundry room, poured in water and made it into *papier-maché*. She then smuggled the few documents and manuscripts that my father needed, hidden in the bottom of a grocery cart, under a pile of carrots and bunches of celery. She smiled and waved at the soldiers in Jeeps lurking on every street corner, machine guns pointed at everyone and everything. If anyone asked, she would make a cute Red Riding Hood reference, joking that she was taking food to her grandmother. And if they had searched her? She would have disappeared into the dark cellar of a secret police torture center.

The closest she ever came to that darkness was a few weeks later, when two agents of the Chilean Gestapo, both in black suits, pulled her into their car, and squeezed her between them behind tinted windows. She had just left an embassy where my father was hiding, and they wanted to know if anyone was staying there. Apparently, a nosy neighbor had seen my father's face from afar as he peeked out a window and mistook it for Carlos Altamirano's, the number one public enemy and head of the Socialist Party who was still on the run at the time. A tall, skinny man, he was built very much like my father and always sported thick dark-rimmed glasses. My mother told me many years later that she pretended to be the English tutor to the ambassador's children, which was a half-truth, since she was an English teacher. When they asked where her husband was, she smirked and said that he was at the beach, writing and drinking with his buddies and doing who knows what.

"You know . . . men," she said with what I can only imagine was a very convincing eye roll and a dismissive shake of the head.

My mother is fearless, and that also can be dangerous. If those agents were not so preoccupied with finding that elusive fugitive and losing the forest for the trees, they would have taken my mother prisoner precisely because she showed no fear. Fear, after all, was the currency of the coming dictatorship. As they often did, they would come looking for the son, for example, and then also take the mother along and torture her, knowing full well she was innocent. The reason was to terrorize the population into submission during those days filled with rumors of tragic deaths and unspeakable horrors whispered by maids sweeping the sidewalks early in the morning, shaking their heads in disbelief. Fear was allowed to invade and occupy the public spaces once freely shared with others, making it impossible to express one's true feelings in public. The repression, the enraged helplessness seeped into the smallest of life's details, an old shoe on a rainy day, the trembling handshake of a friend as he lowered his eyes, lovers on a bench, the cough of a child, the street renamed after a general, the neighbor who never came to visit anymore, the way your face looked after you shaved your beard and put on a tie, every little detail branding the soul into submission. Even back home, after a hard day's work, in the safe privacy of the bedroom, where feelings can be finally confessed to the dark warmth of a lover, the water torture still continued, every drop a constant reminder of the terrible things one did in order to survive. This was the fate that awaited us if we stayed in Chile.

I had my first taste of the life I left behind, had we not gone into exile, when one morning a few days after the coup, while waiting for a bus with my mother, I start humming one of the hymns of the Chilean revolution:

> *Venceremos, venceremos,*
> *mil cadenas habrá que romper,*
> *venceremos, venceremos,*
> *al fascismo sabremos vencer.*

We shall overcome, it says, a thousand chains we will break and, in the end, we will defeat fascism. To be honest, I don't remember this episode at all, but it is now part of the official family lore, since my father wrote it into his memoirs. My mother immediately stopped me and said, or so the story goes, that I should not sing those songs anymore. I stubbornly refused. I was born into revolution, and now my mother was asking me to abort all those years, to suppress and repress the milk of my childhood, to be silent, to be afraid. Those were terrible times, and all of a sudden, we had to grow up very quickly in order to survive them. Now I know that, as in Brecht's terrifying little play *The Informer*, about life in Nazi Germany, many children unconsciously betrayed their parents during those days of the coup. I could have been one of them. She must have grabbed me tightly by the arms and looked into my stubborn little eyes, seen herself and my father in them and decided to tell me the truth.

"If you ever sing those songs again, they will kill your daddy," she warned, point blank.

I can't blame her for her harshness and practicality. And I can't blame myself for forgetting and now for remembering again. Now I know that even back then, as a six-year-old caught in the grip of history, listening to my mother's inevitable request to silence the songs of my childhood, I was unconsciously laying down a strategy for survival.

"But, I can still sing them in my head, can't I?" I answered back.

I knew, don't ask me how, that I wasn't going to let Pinochet infiltrate the banished texture of my skin that easily. I wasn't going to let him twist my life and defeat my heart into bitterness. I wasn't going to let him flood my soul with that torrent of fear. For better or for worse, this foundational memory became the defining moment of my relationship with Chile. A fairy tale told in exile of the imaginary lives I was about to embrace and the floating castles made of songs I chose to build along the way. Stability and flexibility. Every stone filled with the magic of a child discovering the world for the first time. Every song a gentle reminder of where I came from. Full of innocent dreams, it was a place where my memories would reside for a while, where the traumas of my interrupted childhood could sleep at night, safe, undisturbed. Wild and free, those castles would float over the earth with me, from country to country, language to language, life to life.

I left one month after the military coup. With not much more than a stuffed rabbit in one hand and holding onto my mother with the other, I was dragged into exile, seduced by the thrill of flying on airplanes and visiting faraway places, reassured that I would soon return, very soon, to see my country, family, friends, my toys and the life I was leaving behind. Little did we know back then that it would take us ten years to make our first attempt to return home. Like Odysseus, we were destined to roam the earth, clinging like shipwrecks to the flotsam and jetsam of a Chilean revolution which once was but would never be again.

My muse, my fury, my identity sealed and stamped with that curse, with that blessing, with that irresistible myth: the eternal return.

THE GREAT ESCAPE
(Argentina, 1973-1974)

It's always the same. If it's a good night, the clock is ticking. I'm frantically packing a suitcase that refuses to be packed. It magically spits out any garment, shoe or book I'm desperately trying to shove into it. I'm madly dashing by car, bus, bicycle— anything I can get my hands on, anxiously trying to reach the airport and make the flight.

And I never make it. Never.

If it's a bad night, I'm running in the streets of Santiago, chased by soldiers with guns who want to kill me. I wake up in a panic. These two recurring dreams haunted me ever since our escape from Chile, engrained, like deep grooves of a record redirecting the needle to play the same song over and over again, shaping the way I experienced the world around me. It took me decades to realize that anyone can become a prisoner of the metaphors and the stories they tell about themselves, especially when they act them out as if their life depends on it. I was both trapped and escaping at the same time. Amazingly, that tension, that destructive dynamic would empower me to survive the coming injuries of exile.

After all, exile was part of a long family tradition on my father's side of the family. His mother, Fanny Zelicovich, fled with her family after a series of bloody pogroms in Kishinev (today in the Republic of Moldova). When his father, Adolfo Dorfman, was

19

two years old, his family escaped their creditors in Odessa, Greater Russia, in 1909, for a fresh new start in Buenos Aires, Argentina. To complicate matters, Adolfo and his mother Raissa returned to Russia in the summer of 1914 for a visit that turned into a seven-year-long ordeal when the first World War broke out and they were trapped by advancing armies, the Russian Revolution and a bloody civil war. They barely escaped in the early Spring of 1921, via Constantinople, just as famine and a typhus epidemic was decimating their port city of Odessa, killing more than five million people in that region. My grandfather Adolfo probably learned how to be a troublemaker from his mother Raissa, who had been Trotsky's interpreter at Brest-Litovsk during those Russian years. He followed in her footsteps by embracing Marxism, like millions of intellectuals of his generation, flirting with utopia as he became an industrial engineer in his adopted country of Argentina. Now, if he had been a nice Jewish doctor . . . but his politics, his lack of religious beliefs, did not put him in the good graces of Fanny's more traditional family. "No matter," my grandmother once told me, "he was dashing and handsome and rowed me off my feet," as we drank chai in her Buenos Aires kitchen during one of the many times I was able to visit them in the late 1980s.

One sunny Sunday afternoon in the mid-1930s, she was on a date with a nice Jewish doctor who was paddling her in a small boat to an island in the River Plate, a large estuary flowing between Argentina and Uruguay, when my grandfather, who was on the rowing team of the University of Buenos Aires, caught up to them. He must have made quite an impression, because he convinced my grandmother to leave that doctor behind and escape with him back to shore, to live a life my grandmother never imagined she would have. In 1943, a year after my father's birth, a pro-Axis military coup toppled the already conservative Argentine government of Ramón Castillo. When the military took over the University of La Plata, where my grandfather was teaching, that "Jew-dog troublemaker" Adolfo Dorfman, as the papers called him, not only resigned his post, but published the kind of blistering letter that only wins you a kangaroo court and a one-way ticket back to Russia. At that point, family stories intersect, and I don't know if it was Adolfo who fled through the rooftops of Buenos Aires or if it was my Chilean grandfather on my mother's side, Humberto Malinarich, a journalist, who had to escape through the Santiago rooftop, when President Gabriel González Videla, his own godfather, outlawed the Communist Party in 1948.

Maybe they both did?

No matter. It's the kind of fantastic family tale that gives me some consolation when I try to understand why I got expelled at least once from every French school I ever attended. When you grow up in a family of writers, mythmaking becomes second nature. My grandfather Adolfo was a firebrand, but he was no fool. Sensing the coming political turmoil, he had previously applied for a Guggenheim Fellowship in New York, and in keeping with our family's tradition of making generous bets, received the Guggenheim and fled to New York in 1943 to avoid certain imprisonment and deportation back to Odessa. Fanny, my father and his older sister Eleonora joined him a year later, and the family finally reunited and settled in a small apartment on Morningside Drive in Upper Manhattan. Ten years after that, in 1954, thanks to Senator Eugene Joseph McCarthy and the geopolitical perversions of the Cold War, they were forced to escape again, this time to Chile, where my father became possibly an even worse troublemaker, and ten years later found himself hiding in the Argentine Embassy after yet another military coup. Welcome to our cursed family tree.

By the time I celebrated my seventh birthday in Buenos Aires on February 11, 1974, with a trip to an amusement park and a screening of the Beatles' *Yellow Submarine,* things seemed a bit better. All in all, except for recurring nightmares of being chased by men with guns who wanted to kill me, a few traumatic encounters at a day camp with a goose that ate my lunch and some kids punching me and calling me a dirty Jew, I think I must have been pretty happy. Another escape was not on the radar, and my mother made sure I had a semblance of stability while we waited through November for my father's release. My father finally found a way to let the Chilean junta and the Argentinians negotiate a safe passage out of the Argentine Embassy and onto a plane in early December 1973. All I cared about at that point was that my family was together again and that I hadn't gone to school since the previous September. I learned how to read in the company of the classic comic strip *Mafalda* as I was enjoying a five-month holiday, the ultimate childhood fantasy, and that was fine with me. What I didn't know was that the heads of my father's political party had decided to send him to France to organize the Chilean cultural resistance against the dictatorship in exile. Unfortunately, we were stuck in Buenos Aires because my father did not have the appropriate travel documents to leave the country. During the Argentine Embassy days, following the coup, the Chilean government refused to issue my father a passport, and he had stubbornly refused to accept formal refugee status from the United Nations, which would have made our lives considerably easier. Instead, he was betting on reclaiming his long-lost Argentine citizenship while flipping a big giant bird at the Chilean military.

Now that he was in Argentina the bet was not paying off: the local authorities would not recognize his Argentinian birth certificate, and so we were trapped in a situation that my father described in his memoirs as making Kafka look like a realist. Meanwhile, behind the scenes, the wheels of history were slowly grinding, turning Argentina into a death trap. President Juan Perón, who was one of the shadow figures behind the 1943 coup that forced my grandfather into exile in the United States, was now back in power again, this time not accompanied by Evita in a stirring duet, but with his third wife Isabel as vice-president and with Jose López Rega, a Rasputin-like personal secretary obsessed with occultism and divination. Unfortunately, he was also the founder of the Triple A, the Argentinian Anticommunist Alliance, a secret state sponsored paramilitary organization obsessed with killing communists and subversives. It didn't help that on February the 12th, a day after my birthday, the whole country was on edge after a failed assassination attempt against Perón. Meanwhile, the Triple A mission aligned perfectly with the emerging and now infamous Plan Condor, a program created by the military governments of Chile, Paraguay, Bolivia and Brazil to coordinate information on their enemies across borders and kill or disappear them accordingly. In Argentina alone, 30,000 deaths have been attributed to this paramilitary activity. Luckily, one of them was not my father. Fate intervened again, and a family friend facilitated an interview with the police commissioner, who turned out to be more of a lover of literature than a fascist, and a passport was issued within days. By the time we had safely escaped to Lima, Peru, a week or so after my birthday, a death squad came knocking on my great-grandmother Raissa's apartment door in Buenos Aires. She must have bit her tongue and played stupid, because under any other circumstances I'm sure she would have hit them over their heads with her umbrella the way she once did to the chauffeur of a taxi who turned out to be a tsarist émigré in Uruguay. The car almost crashed. But this time the stakes were too high for her to indulge in past grudges. This was life and death.

My only memory of this mythical woman who took the twentieth century by storm and survived is her sitting in her dimly lighted apartment in Buenos Aires, no lightbulbs, just the soft filtered light through her black lace curtains delineating what seemed like rivers of wrinkles pouring out of her face and off her hands into the cup of chai she was silently stirring. Sometimes she would mutter something in Russian. I would just crumble more crackers into my teacup and sit there, content to be in her presence. I have often imagined her transported back to those terrible days of the Russian civil war, finding a quiet moment between storms of Cossack mercenaries and invading foreign armies, watching her son Adolfo drink chai just like I was, or would be, sixty years later, both of us innocently trapped in a history not of our own making, both of us waiting to leave our lives behind and escape again and again into the unknown.

"It's going to be all right," I imagine her saying to her little Adolfo. "It's going to be all right."

EXILE

(Havana, Paris, Amsterdam, Bethesda, 1973-1983)

Sometimes, awake in the dark, I try to imagine that precise moment in time when my exile began. I close my eyes and I see myself at the airport in Santiago on All Saints Day, November 1, 1973, as I go through a military security checkpoint while holding my mother's hand. There are the cold stares of men in steel helmets holding machine guns; a thick layer of dread haunts the terminal. Just like in the movies, we tell ourselves, as if recalling a fantasy is necessary to make it more realistic. As we pass through the metal detector, I hand over my stuffed rabbit to a soldier and demand that he search it. I want to feel like I'm participating too. He smiles and takes it. Do I register the anxiety in my mother's eyes? I doubt it. I have no idea that she doesn't know whether or not her name is on a list, whether in an instant she will be escorted to a back room and possibly never be seen again. It's a classic headline: innocent child delays escape just long enough for family to get caught. Or not. The soldier plays along and pretends to search my rabbit with a "let's see what this rabbit is hiding." Maybe he has a son like me at home, a son he hasn't seen since he was called back to duty as a reservist after the coup, and he misses him, just like I miss my father. Maybe he's seen and done things he would rather forget, and this momentary pause makes him feel human again? I would love to put my finger on this moment of empathy as the birth of my exile, as if I was taking along with me a road map for reconciliation pointing to a return without bitterness. But, I can't. It's too early and too nicely wrapped and convenient to contain all the complexities of my coming journey.

There are still many more borders to cross, I tell myself in the dark.

I'm in bed, still awake. My wife, Primm, sleeps with her head resting on my shoulder while her purring cats surround us with their desperate need for love. My body sinks into the memory foam under the sheets, and I'm lost in this imaginary childhood game I used to play, right around September of 1974. After a year of bouncing from country to country, living out of our suitcases and then slogging through a miserable never-ending summer in Paris in more dingy hotels and borrowed apartments than I can remember, we've settled in Palaiseau, a quiet suburb on the outskirts of Paris. My parents have rented a small house with a picture-perfect backyard, a clothesline and a blossoming cherry tree. There are even hints that we'll get a rabbit. We've found a real stable home and with that home a nearby school and the inevitable realization that my one-year holiday is finally coming to an end. I am now ready, like a conscript, to join the rest of humanity and march to a time measured by bells, rigid schedules and military-like discipline. I hate school and I hate getting up in the mornings and I hate having to go to sleep at night when my mind is still speeding like a pinball bouncing in ten different directions at once.

Around this time, I get rid of my night-light and embrace my fear of the dark. Of course, I'm still afraid of walking into a pitch-dark room where I easily conjure up monsters and murderers ready to jump out and kill me from some hidden corner. Even in my own home. But once we finish our nightly safari hunt for those blood sucking French mosquitos, smashing them with a rolled-up *Paris Match,* and my father tells me a bedtime story and my mother kisses me good night and the door shuts behind them, I am now ready to be left in total darkness for the first time in my life. When I close my eyes, I discover something magical:

traces of bright incandescent lights radiating from the back of my eyelids, like a film projection. It's as if the screen of the universe has been pierced by a million pins as bright as the sun. Today, I know there is a scientific explanation for this phenomenon; these patterns that look like an ocean of mercury are called phosphenes and, according to a quick search on the Internet, are believed to be caused by "the natural electrical charges the retina produces when it's in a resting state." Fortunately for me, when I was seven years old, the Internet did not exist, and I can still live in a world where readily available scientific explanations do not ruin my appreciation for the magic and the fantasy of my everyday life. I truly believe I am astro-projecting myself into another dimension, time traveling into the past and conjuring up memory after memory of my days gone by as if watching, directing and starring in the movie of my life. I call it el Juego de la memoria, "the Memory Game," and it becomes the only way I can fall asleep on a school night. In the game, I recall past birthdays and holidays, what I did the day before, my first encounter with Roman and Greek ruins, when I ran the entire length of the Circus Maximus at night, all by myself, on a bet for a Mars bar, with the ghost of Ben-Hur and the echoes of a hundred thousand screaming Romans trailing beside me, while my father holds a secret meeting with a member of the Chilean resistance. There are also sleepless nights when I sneak downstairs to the basement, where my albino rabbit Garibaldi is staying. Writer and family friend Julio Cortázar has left him in our care for a few summer months while he travels with his family. I'm fascinated. I turn on the bare lightbulb and stare at him. His bright red eyes stare back at me, without a single blink, nothing. I sit there, like a mule, waiting until dawn, and I am suddenly exhausted. I go upstairs to find my father in the kitchen with his café con leche and his green Olivetti typewriter. I tell him that I have spent the whole night waiting for Garibaldi to fall asleep and that I am too tired to go to school. He shakes his head: I have to go to school. That is the worse day ever, as my daughters Catalina and Isabella love to say. But, even if I had known that rabbits have three eyelids and that one of them is a thin transparent membrane that keeps the eyes moist, allowing them to pretend to be awake, I would have waited regardless, because I was born to be a contrarian.

And then there were those precious few months we spent in Cuba, right between our escape from Buenos Aires and our arrival in France in May of 1974. We were guests of the Cuban government, staying on the 20th floor of the Havana Libre, formerly known as the Havana Hilton. This is where I discovered *tutti frutti* ice cream, spent hours going up and down fancy elevators and saw my first cabaret performance with women dancing the mambo, sporting long vivid multi-colored feathers and revealing sequined outfits. I remember one of them winking at me while flying on a trapeze. I blushed. Havana is where I met Hyadée Santamaría, the legendary icon of the Cuban Revolution who had been at the assault on the legendary Moncada fortress; she had been imprisoned with Fidel, then fought alongside him in the Sierra Maestra and became the founder of Casa de Las Américas, a cultural institution home to a myriad of dissident artistic voices from Latin America, including my father's. She gave me a guerilla uniform worn by the Communist Youth Brigades. I also remember Beba, who took time from her busy schedule running Casa de las Américas like a swiss clock to measure my torn-up disheveled stuffed rabbit and make a replica, cutting and sewing it back to life right in front of me during one long afternoon. She was gentle, her voice was sharp but also soothing, and she made me feel special. The revolutions of the twentieth century, for all their faults, shared one thing in common: children were the center of attention.

My grandfather Adolfo, whenever he described the harsh living conditions in Odessa during the Russian Civil War, would tell me how the city would sometimes change hands in the course of a single day, back and forth between the French invading armies, the White Cossacks and the Red Army. He would go to school with bullets flying.

"And do you know how I knew if the Communists were in charge of the city that day?" he would ask me between puffs of his pipe gently rocking himself in his favorite wicker chair. "The children were the first ones to be fed. Always."

Those moments stayed with my grandfather for the rest of his life, and I'm sure they influenced his future political allegiances. He never forgot. Just as I will never forgot how the Cuban Revolution and its people offered me a momentary refuge in what had been a traumatic year. I had no way of knowing that a few miles from the relative luxury of the Havana Libre, Reynaldo Arenas, the untamed and surreal Cuban writer, was being jailed, along with so many others, in the infamous El Morro Prison for being a homosexual and a dissident. For years, I lived ignorant of that cruel contradiction. For millions of left-wing activists, the Cuban Revolution represented an ideal of self-determination and social justice that was tragically absent from the rest of the American continent at that time. The very real advancements of the Cuban Revolution in the fields of health care and education (compared to the failures of the United States) that effectively brought millions of poor peasants into a dignified existence was enough for many to brush aside the issue of human rights violations. The truth is that, at that point in history, my temporary paradise was Reynaldo Arenas' living hell. But, of course, my memories today, during my nighttime insomnia, are not the memories of a seven-year-old desperately in need of romanticizing his experience of the world in simple black and white in order to survive, night after night, memory after memory, and finally find a way to put them to bed and fall asleep in a foreign land.

But that was not it either. That memory game of double exposures between the past and the present, my lost home in Chile and my new one in France, between my dreams and reality that experience of nostalgia before I even knew what nostalgia was does not ring true enough to the moment I'm searching for. In this mapping of my memories of exile, deep and wide, in this labyrinth inside my castle, still awake at night after all these years, I know there's one missing moment, one treasure so special my mother called it *un milagro,* a miracle when it happened. When I recently asked her about that elusive moment, she told me it reminded her of the scene in *Gone with the Wind* when Vivien Leigh sinks to her knees in a ravaged field and raises her fist to the heavens, a blood red sunset behind her, declaring with her savage will to survive that she'll never be hungry again. This Vivien Leigh moment is buried so deep in my subconscious, covered in so many layers of sweet revenge and calculated necessity, enveloped in a shroud of such anger and magnificent pride that I don't think I'll ever be able to precisely conjure it up to the surface of these pages.

This much is clear, my father was exiled because he made a clear choice: to follow in the footsteps of his revolutionary ancestors. I was never given that choice. In the eyes of the world, I was a victim of the Pinochet regime and a victim of circumstances. It was a mask that grew on me like a second skin, slowly, insidiously and naturally seducing me with its poisoned powers. Before I search around the far edges of this treasure chest that contains the moment I refused to be seen as more than just a victim sealed and hidden in the darkest corners of my imaginary castle during that summer of 1974, on the heels of our arrival in Paris I must return to a butcher shop where my mother is trying to buy some sliced ham.

The shop was busy, filled with rude French people elbowing each other. I was so small, all I could see was a jungle of feet tussling and stepping on each other's toes to get near the counter, where the butcher stood holding court, barking orders to his assistants who were feverishly cutting and wrapping what I can only imagine now, after twelve years of French education, were sausages, *terrines, ballotines, rillettes, andouilles, boudin* and, yes, *jambon* (ham). To me, it was all cacophony; I didn't know a single word of French and I might as well have been somewhere in China or Saudi Arabia. At the time, we were staying in a low-rent hotel with a small kitchenette, the perfect destination for recently arrived third-world immigrants. It was dark, dingy and dirty; the back windows opened into a large inner courtyard blackened by the centuries where you could hear Spanish, Portuguese, Arabic and even Swahili rise from its depths, mixed in with the aromas of fried foods and exotic spices. My nose bled every night and in the mornings I would wake up, as in a horror movie, my pillow soaked in blood, and the maid would come in and complain out loud about it with all the guttural hate and spite her xenophobia could muster. The oil crisis of 1973 had hit France hard, and with it came a wave of anti-immigrant laws targeting the influx of migrants coming from France's lost colonies. We were dirty foreigners, and she was going to make us pay for it. Just like the butcher.

It was finally my mother's turn, and he pointed at her to speak up.

"'*Dou yanbon, s'il vous plait*,'" she says, mispronouncing the word for ham.

My mom knew how to read French from her university studies but spoke with a heavy accent.

The butcher said something like, "I don't understand," and made my mother repeat y*ambon* again in front of everyone, as he watched with morbid curiosity. She repeated it a couple more times, but the butcher, like a cat toying with a mouse, kept the game going, making sure my mother paid for her linguistic transgressions and understood one of the most fundamental lessons for any recently arrived immigrant: if you can't speak proper French (and like my mother, you're not white), you're a third-class citizen and you should expect to be treated as such.

Someone in a rush to place an order shouted in perfect French, "The lady wants *du jambon*, and let's get on with it!"

The butcher mockingly repeated the word *jambon*, emphasizing perfectly the "j" sound at the beginning of the word, and then barked the order to his faithful servants. Anyone acquainted with my mother knows that she has the power and the spirit to bring down giants. I can only imagine how hard it is for her to have stood there silently and be publicly humiliated by this man who was old enough to have been a Nazi collaborator during the German occupation, selling his choice meats to the SS officers who in turn let him run his black-market business on the side. As I mature, I have come to know his type all too well; one just like him ran the French middle school I attended in the late '70s in the Hague, when we lived in Amsterdam. He claimed to have escaped from a German labor camp and hiked all the way to Norway and then back to France after the war, but when he closed the doors of his office, he beat children with a cane.

The majority of the French in positions of authority that I encountered in my childhood disliked children. They must have held to that steadfast medieval belief that children were nothing more than miniature adults who could only learn discipline through fear and punishment. This oppressive culture, for better or for worse, became an essential part of the universe of my rebellious childhood.

When my parents attempted to enroll me in the local school up the street from our new rental house in a quiet suburb of Paris, they were told that I should go instead to a special school for migrant and refugee children who didn't speak French; it was a school my mother described as a dead-end segregated institution where children were left to be forgotten. Though I imagine she was exaggerating, my parents concluded that the best thing for me was to go to school with the other French children in the neighborhood, so that I could begin to have the contours of a "normal" life again. Putting aside the few months I spent at the Latinoamericano in Santiago, I had never gone to school and I had never officially learned to read and write.

My mother, the tireless archivist of the family, has kept every single one of my school reports since 1974, and recently she shared them with me as a gift inside a thick yellow manila envelope with the words "Dorfman Dossier" written on them. My mother has a peculiar sense of humor. She also has kept my first notebook and the first set of tests I took in class, which consisted of blank pages and big, fat red-inked zeros at the bottom. There I was, the only immigrant, test after test sitting, powerless, in that classroom, staring at those blank pages, watching the other boys and girls scribble down the answers of a test I could not even understand. I remember that the teacher would then read out loud the names of the students and their corresponding grades, deliberately and dramatically emphasizing the worst and the best scores. I will never forget the way my last name was pronounced in French: Dorfman with the guttural French "r" making it sound like a death sentence. All this was accompanied by a Greek chorus of ooohs and aaahs from the students hanging on to every syllable, like vultures on dead meat in a perfectly executed ancient ritual of shaming. I'll be honest, I probably deserved the zero. If I was going to be in a French school without any support or resources for someone like me, why should I expect to be treated any differently from the other kids? I wanted to be in a French school without knowing French? If I wanted to be "normal" and cheat reality, then I was going to have to pay the humiliating price of belonging to a culture that wasn't mine. It was a price that would forever change the course of my life.

Who am I? Where is home? Where do I belong?

The experiences of exile and migration have that rare luminous quality that can transform apparently abstract existential questions into a series of practical challenges that everyone at some point in their lives has to confront. Should my children be born in this faraway land? What language will I speak to them? Should I buy a home? Should I return to the place of my birth? Who will take care of my parents? Where should I be buried? As I grew older and encountered more of these existential crossroads in myself and stories of others, my tendency to run right past the cautionary stop signs of life and rush forward propelled by the sheer force of necessity and the need to survive was tempered by the number of very real scars on my wounded body and mind.

But when you're seven, you don't stop to reflect about the choices you make for yourself. I chose to surrender to a foreign language and learn French from one day to the next. Literally.

I'll show them, I emphatically declared to my parents one angry afternoon. Never again was I going to allow another zero, another public shaming to humiliate me that way. I was going to speak French better than the French. I was going to master every guttural "r" and placement of the tongue and intonation of this new language. I made a choice to let it in, so that French could live side by side with the language of my Chilean childhood.

I had been bilingual once before, on another planet, in another lifetime. In early 1968, my father received a fellowship to finish a book on Latin American literature at the University of California, Berkeley. We landed at ground zero of the counter-culture revolution sweeping through the United States and much of the Western world, and I plunged right into that beautiful madness. Between the ages of one and two and half, I spoke Spanglish as my first language with a smattering of such pure English expressions as "choo-choo train" and "Peace now! LSD!" It was the usual fare, I'm sure, for any toddler hanging out in People's Park or running up and down the green lawns of Golden Gate Park in the Summer of 1968 to the sounds of Jefferson Airplane and Janis Joplin. By the time we returned to Chile in mid-1969, I had forgotten my psychedelic gringo adventure and became monolingual again as the English language retreated to the backwaters of my mind.

Could my early bilingual adventures be one of the reasons I was so receptive to learning French so quickly, defying any scientific explanation? Looking at my monthly report cards from 1974, I can trace a clear timeline. At the end of the first month, I was declared absent from spelling and creative writing, I had an F in history and science, an A in reading and recitation and an A+ in mathematics. So, I could read and recite short poems from memory, but I had no idea what I was saying or writing. And obviously I could do numbers, I could do math. I was basically faking it until I could make it. By the next report card, I had a C average in creative writing, spelling, history and science. In one month, I had learned enough French to be an average but fluent French student and stay afloat enough to graduate to second grade. I was never able to master using an ink pen, since I was left-handed and my notebooks were blotched like the edges of a Jackson Pollock, even though I would twist myself into a pretzel to avoid smudging the ink. The result was that I was now fluent enough in French to stand up for myself.

I could not be in Chile to resist the Pinochet dictatorship, so I must have transferred the anger boiling inside me and used it to rebel against a repressive educational system that wanted to box me into a square, when all I wanted was to be as a circle. *Zero de conduite* (Zero for Conduct), as in Jean Vigo's famous (and banned) 1933 film depicting the rebellious and anarchist spirit of a group of young French students in a boarding school or Truffaut's *The 400 Blows* or even Lindsay Anderson's *If*. My tongue became my sword, and I entered into battle as if my life depended on it.

At the center of this youthful rebellion was a piece of cheese. Not any kind of cheese, not the harmless garden-variety mozzarella or provolone, but a stinky, foul-smelling, disgusting little piece of French cheese. Thanks to the French welfare state, I was on the free lunch program because our family's income at the time was below the poverty line. My mother worked sporadically as an English tutor, and my father was applying for every possible grant and fellowship he could find while working for free to organize the Chilean resistance against the dictatorship. And so, every day, I enjoyed a delicious free lunch in the school cafeteria, served by these jolly old ladies who cooked it for us from scratch. Unfortunately, the French, being French, served a piece of cheese at the end of most meals and, like every other normal French kid, I was expected to eat it, especially since I was eating for free. Tragically, I was totally, completely and utterly disgusted by the smell.

Maybe I can blame my grandfather Adolfo who was a lover of putrid rotten cheeses with worms and hues of the bubonic plague. He thought Roquefort was mild. I remember going shopping with him in Santiago, before the coup, to a cheese store where we had to step over wet sawdust and dead flies to get to the counter. There, on display under majestic glass cheese domes, lay a foul pantheon of rankness that traumatized me for the rest of my life.

At lunch in the school cafeteria, I made sure to sit next to the kid who loved stinky cheese so that I could pass it under the table while none of the *surveillants,* were watching. Two tall men would pace up and down between the rows of tables to make sure that no one shared their food. "No sharing!" they shouted, one of them pointing his particularly long index finger at us. I know that when you're small, everything seems to be so big—rooms, houses—and then you return one day as an adult, and you're like, I thought it was so much bigger! I believe if today I saw this *surveillant*, whom I will call Monsieur Lecon, who is probably dead now, his index finger would still make an impression on me. I visualize it today in a wide-angle lens, inches away from my nose as I turn my little head around and up to face him. One day, I hadn't been able to smuggle my cheese, while the rest of the kids had almost finished theirs and the recess bell was about to ring.

"*Mange*," eat, the finger said.

I stared back at him, and my eyes must have said it all as I looked down at the plate I had pushed as far away from me as my arms could stretch. I put my elbows on the table, sank my fists into my cheeks and said nothing.

He bent over me, put his hands and his long fingers on the table and, almost whispering in my ear, said, "If you don't eat it, you'll have to stay here and miss recess."

The bell rang. Children filed out one by one from their tables like inmates in a prison. The cafeteria emptied and the last shuffling footsteps could be heard echoing down the corridor as I remained steadfast in my chair with my rebellious mind and my plate of cheese.

Monsieur Lecon pulled out a chair and sat himself down in front of me. He pushed the plate to me, and I pushed it back. He pushed it again unsuccessfully a few more times, then gave up. "*Mange ton fromage*," he said, now clearly annoyed. Eat your cheese.

He nervously tapped his fingers on the table. I remember being fascinated, thinking they looked just like the legs of a hairy spider. My mind wandered off for a few seconds only to be brought back to life by the increasingly irritated voice of Monsieur Lecon.

"You know, we can stay here as long as it takes, and you will miss the whole recess."

I nodded. I was biting my tongue because I didn't feel like getting into more trouble than I was already in, but I couldn't help myself. I was born a smart-ass, and I guess I'll die a smart-ass.

"Well," I said with a loud, insolent, beating heart, "then I guess you're stuck in here with me, and you won't be able to smoke your cigarette."

His face, oh, his face. If I could find the words to describe it! His pencil-thin mustache twitched, a slight tremor registered on his lips and his beady eyes blinked repeatedly under his bushy eyebrows. His hands tensed up. He was probably wishing he could hit me, but he really wanted that cigarette, and the mere reminder of the absence of nicotine was enough to defeat him. He waved his spider-like hand, "*Vas t' en*," get lost, he said.

"*Merci.*" I got the hell out of there.

Later that afternoon, I was pulled out of class and taken to the principal's office. They made you wait. They called my parents, but no one was home. I waited some more, and then my father walked into the room. It wasn't the first time or the last time he had to interrupt his day to get me out of trouble. He stepped into the office. The principal explained the situation: It was simply incomprehensible that Rodrigo did not eat his cheese. "*Ça se fait pas,*" it's just not done. This is France, and when in France, you eat the cheese that you are given. And besides, it's delicious. The kids love it.

The principal was genuinely perplexed. My father tried to explain cultural and gastronomic differences, appealing to his sense of solidarity, and poor exiled Rodrigo this and poor immigrant Rodrigo that. In the end, I got three days' suspension but never had to eat another piece of stinky cheese again.

I had won. Unfortunately, this episode only served to embolden my rebellious identity, and it only got worse after that: hours standing in the corner of the classroom like a prisoner awaiting execution, recesses denied, field trips spent punished sitting on the dirty floor of the boy's bathroom writing, "*On ne parle pas en classe,*" no talking during class, five hundred times over and over again. Every rebellious moment was a badge of honor and a reminder that the revolutionary songs of my childhood had not been forgotten. No, they were living, breathing memories—demanding, shouting from the ramparts and the bell towers that I had to stay true to their ideals of justice and resistance. Too many people had died defending them, too many generations of Dorfmans and Malinarichs had put their lives on the line fighting to make sure that, in the words of Martin Luther King, quoting Theodore Parker, "The arc of the moral universe is long, but it bends towards justice." I was going to fight for every inch of my dignity against a system built to beat it into submission, no matter the consequences.

I don't envy my parents. I was an insolent, disrespectful pain in the ass who was suspended from every single school he ever attended and never learned his lesson. "Don't fight every single battle like it's the only battle left in the world," my parents never grew tired of saying. But what could they do? This was both my medicine and my poison, and they knew it. Unfortunately, I didn't. How could I? I was just a child. It would take me decades to realize that, like Antigone demanding justice for her dead brother, I was willing to walk in a path of self-destruction in the name of upholding an impossible ideal. But, isn't that also the path of the romantic hero? As a child, I treasured reading Howard Fast and watching Spartacus die on the Roman cross as he sees for one last loving time his child born into freedom. I worshipped Butch Cassidy and the Sundance Kid frozen in that sepia photograph with the sounds of ¡Fuego! echoing in my heart and in the movie theatre. I shed tears with Robert Jordan, in Hemingway's *For Whom the Bell Tolls*, as he lies, wounded and dying, waiting to take his last shots so that his *camaradas* can escape into a doomed Republican cause during the Spanish Civil War. Then, of course, the Count of Montecristo with his cold, sweet self-defeating revenge, Che Guevara, and more importantly Chilean president Salvador Allende in that iconic photograph of resistance, with his finger on the trigger of a machine gun, looking up at the fighter jets circling the Presidential Palace. In the end, Allende took his own life, but at the time we refused to believe it, and instead we mystified and glorified his death, in our eyes and our tears and our hunger for martyrs. I fell in love with lost causes because I knew, I somehow *knew* as a seven-year-old that my world, like a phoenix, was born from the ashes of that loss, shaped by the fire of our defeats, nurtured by the memories of those who came before us.

In the darkness, I can now clearly see where it all began. My exile began with a choice: a choice to be the protagonist of my own history.

I was seven and there was no turning back.

THE GOLDEN EXILE

That's how General Pinochet and his propaganda machine denounced our banished lives: "The Golden Exile." We were living like millionaires, the military shouted from their Jeeps; filet mignon sizzling on barbecue grills, they screamed inside their torture chambers; whiskey and Cuban cigars, their talking heads denounced on the evening news, while everyone in Chile had to eat shit.

I have to admit that exile had indeed been a privilege, all the pain and all the joy carved on the skin of my Chilean identity, festering a thousand reasons in the minds of those who had stayed behind to resent our exile and mistrust our return.

When you're young and romantic and you hear the words "next year in Jerusalem," you think of paradise. When you recall the smell of sliced tomatoes in Santiago, you tremble, your mind wanders off like a condor soaring above the eternal snow caps of the Andes, dipping my wings into the savage and embryonic waters of the Pacific. Exile tunes your heart to receive the far away clichés of your country as if they were the sweetest of imaginary fragrances. It turns an *empanada* freshly baked in Amsterdam into the whole of Chile to be devoured according to the hunger of your nostalgia. *Empanada* in hand, I would sometimes watch some of my Chilean *compatriotas* nibble, some cry, some eat it whole, and others slowly chew, lost in reverie, every bite, a step closer (and of course, a step back) from that farawayland.

By the time I was getting ready to leave Amsterdam in 1981 for the United States and throw those precious marbles out the window, I was speaking French in school and street Dutch with my neighborhood friends. I had learned English watching *Benny Hill* and *I, Claudius* on the BBC, and most important of all, I spoke Spanish at home. As a child of exile, I had the opportunity to reinvent myself a thousand times over, inhabiting, if I wanted, the suave designer shoes of a tasty little Frenchman, perhaps taking on the rosy cheeks of a Dutch boy full of milk or masquerading myself later in the United States as the imaginary naive, exuberant all-American kid with a football and a twang. You name it, I could have been that . . . and I probably was.

For all the pain there was also a lot of joy, especially once we escaped Paris in 1976 and moved to Amsterdam, where my father finally found a stable job teaching Latin American literature at the University of Amsterdam. Exile was an adventure where I could travel by myself across Amsterdam on a bicycle or hop on a tram, free to roam its cobblestone streets and canals, and even skate on its ice-covered sidewalks during those interminable Northern European winters, straight out of a Breughel painting, before the days of global warming. I played in a soccer youth league and learned how to slide and tackle the ball on perfectly soft green fields, learned how to cuss in Dutch, collect stamps and, of course, play marbles. And the members of the Chilean solidarity movement welcomed us with open arms, offering us their homes, their used furniture, their time and their friendship. They had names I had never heard or pronounced before: Jasja, Bert, Martje, Minneke. The Dutch most certainly fit the hard-nosed, Northern protestant stereotype, but our friends, who loved Chile and were still inspired by the spirit of the Chilean revolution, were also strangely very Latin American. They had this casual lightheartedness about punctuality and social mores that made them charming and intriguing. In the summers, with the help of my visiting grandparents Adolfo and Fanny, we were able to afford holidays in Tunisia, where I rode a camel pretending I was Lawrence of Arabia and befriended Sophia Loren's son, Carlo Ponti Jr. and tried hard not to ogle his mother while she rode on her paddle boat in swanky Mahamat Beach. In Italy, I peed, just like my father did in 1951, on the steps of the Vatican because they wouldn't let us use their bathroom and drove a small motorboat by myself through the canals of Venice. Then there was Yugoslavia and Romania and Greece and the Peloponnese and Crete and the ruins of Knossos. There wasn't a single public square with pigeons I did not terrorize, not a single monument I did not climb, not a ruin I did not play hide and seek in. There was a palpable split personality syndrome in our lives during those European years as we transitioned from being tourists in the summer back to being immigrants in an unforgiving Paris or a cold and frozen Amsterdam.

At the same time, when you get whacked by history, your pendulum tends to swing long and wide between hope and despair, between the masking and the unmasking of your fears and desires. It's easy to be crushed by the weight of historical circumstances, like a crowd running from a collapsing building. The first instinct is to run, forget and never look back.

I had constructed a castle to encompass the whole of the Spanish language. I was going to rescue my mother tongue from the jaws of the dragon of Babel, from disappearing into the fiery belly of all those other languages I was absorbing. Part of me was still standing at the castle gate, making sure that the music and the lights and the laughter of my new immigrant songs would never compromise the integrity of the songs of my Chilean childhood.

I remember my proud parents asking me to demonstrate my linguistic dexterity to the many *tíos* passing through our house over those years, and I remember steadfastly refusing their requests. Not out of shyness, but more out of shame. I instinctively knew that all those languages inside of me, no matter how much I enjoyed speaking them, still carried the seeds of my possible betrayal. I did not want to lose the songs I had made for myself in those early days when we had first left Chile. And the only way to achieve that was to remain in a constant state of suspension, never truly committing or conforming to the demands of the cultures around me. Sometimes I was like Penelope, waiting, chaste to her memories and true to her promises; other times I was Odysseus fighting to resist immersion and the gentle soothing songs of the sirens of exile. "Be normal," they sang, "make one simple choice." I was not swayed. Instead, I took on this dangerous gamble, betting on the future, betting that I could live on the margins, keeping my critical distance, always waiting for that mythical return to Chile that would bring me back to the wonders of my childhood before the coup, before the Great Escape.

It never crossed my mind that such a path could end in total and abject failure and that I could be left with nothing more than the ghost of an identity, roaming the dark halls of a crumbling castle, floating at the edge of nowhere. In exile, the possibility of becoming an empty shell always lurked around the corner. Emptiness, but at least not fear. When the sun rose over Santiago and our friends and family sighed in relief because no one had knocked on their doors at two in the morning, they still had to go to work in a world full of real nightmares, where the wrong word could break a bone, where there was no actual escape from the menacing violence of everyday life. When the sun rose in Paris, it was a rough and sometimes humiliating day for immigrants, but even a homeless Senegalese refugee sleeping on a bench in La Gare du Nord, holding tight to his garbage bag of belongings, had more options than those he'd left behind.

I was of course even more privileged. I was free, free to speak my mind, free to educate myself, free to not be afraid and, ultimately, if I chose, free to re-invent myself completely. I could forget the whole thing, marry a nice French girl and not teach my children another word of Spanish ever again. That was never an option for those who stayed behind in Chile. Their personal schism was rooted in the reality of life under a brutal dictatorship; ours was rooted in the fact that we weren't there, although with every bite of that sacred *empanada*, we imagined ourselves to be.

WELCOME TO AMERICA
(Bethesda, Maryland, 1981-1983)

I don't exactly know the precise moment my mother started plotting against my father's wishes to live in Mexico City while we waited and waited for the end of our exile. Maybe it was while we crossed the Atlantic on that cargo ship, which carried the entirety of our belongings (forty-seven boxes and thirteen suitcases) to a wooden dock in Baltimore, our transitory destination in our slow-motion journey back to South America via Mexico. Or maybe it started after we had rented a small two-story house on Edward Avenue, nestled in the quiet suburb of Bethesda, Maryland, where she finally recognized that she was tired of moving around the world like a dispossessed refugee.

We were all tired. The past seven years had been exhausting, and all my mother wanted was to either stop running or go back to Chile and be with her mother Elba, her two siblings Pato and Ana María and the new nephews and nieces born after the coup. Then, too, there were the countless cousins and uncles in Santa María, the small rural village where she had spent most of her childhood and adolescence. My father, on the other hand, had no family in Chile and he was the only one with the dreaded letter "L" stamped on his Chilean passport. This "L" became a scarlet letter of exile for my father and for the other 30,000 Chileans who, like him, had been officially forbidden to return to Chile. The appearance of this mysterious "L" and its meaning was cause for great speculation among the exiled community, especially since the functionaries at the consulate refused to tell them what it stood for, probably as part of a psych operation meant to inflict as much pain and confusion as possible. "It must mean you're on a *Lista,* a List," my father would say, taking the bait, "but that's too obvious," he would continue, "they're much too perverse to make it that simple." Leave it to a writer to obsessively go down a dark rabbit hole in search of a deeper meaning where there is none. Unfortunately, there was nothing poetic or perverse in this "L". It simply meant "Limited Entry", the perfectly bland and mediocre creation of a government who was literally killing their poets. So, my mother could have returned if she wanted to, but she knew that would have meant breaking up the family and creating another sort of exile.

My father's plan was simple. We would stay in the United States for one year while he negotiated our move to Mexico. He wanted my brother, Joaquín Emiliano Alonso, born in Amsterdam in 1979, to be raised surrounded by his mother tongue and embraced by a vibrant Latin American culture as a way to lessen the impact of our continuing exile on him. Unfortunately, after the coup, Mexico had broken all diplomatic ties with Chile and, ironically, this made it very difficult for us to obtain a residency visa. Julio Sherer, the editor-in-chief of the daily Mexican newspaper *Excélsior* from 1968 to 1975, and then the founder of the influential magazine *Proceso*, had told my father that we would have nothing to worry about and that he would personally get the visa from his old friend José López Portillo, the current president of Mexico.

Meanwhile, my father had finagled a one-year fellowship at the Smithsonian's Woodrow Wilson International Center for Scholars to write *The Last Song of Manuel Sendero*, an outrageous experimental novel, part comic book, part mythical story about a rebellion of fetuses who refuse to be born unless all the adults come together and meet their utopian demands for a perfect world. The madness of my father's writing was present everywhere in our lives. Thinking back to those forty-seven boxes holding every book he had collected in exile and a draft of every novel, poem and essay he had written ever since leaving Chile, and my mother having to hold down the fort of our daily lives, I now realize what a high price we had to pay for his sanity, for our sanity. But back in July 1981 as my father was desperately trying to wrestle a fistful of quarters from his pockets to feed into the payphone on one of the docks of the Port of Baltimore, in order to get our belongings safely to Washington, DC, all I cared about during those first moments on American soil was getting a milkshake and a copy of the latest *Mad Magazine* from the nearby snack bar.

As I slurped my vanilla shake, my father told the incredulous customs agent that we would only be in the United States for a year and then we would move to Mexico City. He pleaded with him to ignore our forty-seven boxes and thirteen suitcases. In one of those lucky twists of fate my family seems to periodically conjure up when all hope is lost, the customs agent, just like that police commissioner in Buenos Aires back in 1974, happened to be a lover of Latin American literature. He had even read the cult classic *Rayuela* (*Hopscotch* in English), the labyrinthian novel written by Julio Cortázar, a book that profoundly influenced my father's writing to this day. In my sugar-induced mind as I watched these two men go down the rabbit hole of books I had never read, all I could think of was that when I was eight years old, Cortázar taught me how to make a rocket-like paper airplane that I immediately proceeded to fly onto philosopher Michel Foucault's unsuspecting, glistening bald head, during the intermission of Chris Marker's film *La Spirale* in a Paris movie house. I was about to insert this intimate memory to the conversation, ready to impress and seal the deal, when the customs agent, no doubt sensing the importance of his historical role in our journey of exile, let our boxes through and welcomed us to the United States of America. My father was back in his childhood home, and I was ready to enter the land of rock 'n' roll and California girls, frozen pizzas and never-ending images flickering past midnight on color televisions.

My parents dutifully arranged their lives around mine and rented a small two-story house a few miles away from my new French high school in unaffordable Bethesda, which was already on its way to becoming the gentrified enclave it is today. My father started on his book and my mother managed the house and our daily lives. I quickly learned to mow the lawn, decipher the mysteries of American football and discover *Happy Days*, *Welcome Back Kotter* and *Hill Street Blues* on American television.

. . . And donuts. Donuts were amazing.

My life was about to significantly improve in another way. When we had moved to Amsterdam from Paris in 1976, it made no sense to switch me to a Dutch school. Amid the upheaval of exile, a French education was going to be one of the principal anchors of my life. Unfortunately for me, the only French middle school in Holland was located in the Hague, a two-hour bus ride from our apartment in the suburbs of Buitenveldert, on the outskirts of Amsterdam. Four hours on a bus every day in a northern country meant that in Winter, I had to get up every morning before the crack of dawn, and in the Spring I had to go to bed while the sun was still shining. I remember how I raged at having to lie in my bunk bed while I heard the squeals of my Dutch friends running around the neighborhood streets without me. To make things worse, my middle school was designed like a prison. It was a gray, stone, turn-of-the-century mansion surrounded by a barbed-wire fence with a desolate courtyard without a blade of grass in sight. There, I suffered the relentless bullying by entitled wealthy French upperclassmen. I hated that school like I hated few things in my life and I would have happily set it on fire. But that was then. Now in the United States, I could sleep late and bike to a high school that felt like paradise with its lush green lawns, soccer field, wide open spaces lined with stately oak trees . . . and there was not a bully in sight.

I went to school with the sons and daughters of the ambassadors and functionaries of the embassies of Zaire, Indonesia, Luxembourg, Belgium, Togo, Senegal, Algeria and the *crème de la crème* of an endless list of organizations such as the IMF and the World Bank. I was well aware that we could only afford for me to go to this private school because my grandparents were paying for it. Intellectually, I was right at home, but economically, I was out of my league, and that was just fine. My parents had always provided what I needed, and I had grown to form a modest approach to wearing brand names and living in a materialistic world. In Europe, for example, I remember my thrifty mother making our lamps from empty jugs of wine. We never bought beds and rarely furniture; they were usually hand-me-downs from the Chilean solidarity network around us. This was both a function of our economic reality and of our exiled minds, demanding that we live out of a suitcase because you never knew when, at a moment's notice, we were going to be able to go back home.

I see this pattern today when I walk into the homes of some of my Mexican immigrant friends who still live in this self-imposed minimalism, the kind that saves them from drowning under the weight of materialism and keeps them afloat in the hopes that one day, sooner than later, they will be able to go back home and renew their unfinished lives with the money saved from toiling in El Norte.

Crossing the Atlantic Ocean had been more of a time traveling adventure for me than a geographical shift. Before I knew it, I was a teenager ready to lose myself in a blaze of adolescent love. Countless poets have spent their entire lives trying to capture the essence of that first kiss, the pounding of the heart and staccato breath that dampens the neck as bodies cautiously embrace, inching closer and closer in a slow dance to *Hotel California* on repeat in the dimly lit basement of a nondescript, split-level suburban house. Nothing could have prepared me for that flood of emotions and its complementary heartbreak. Unconsciously, I discovered that romantic love was no different from my longing for a Chile that was now slowly receding in the distance of my adolescence like a mist or a fog you can never quite reach or even touch with your fingers. I was exalted and euphoric in one single breath and then crushed and betrayed in the next. With every heartbreak, I perfected the art of shameless self-pity. First you must lie in the dark, on your bed, staring at the ceiling. Second, you listen to a particularly sad song, like the Beatles' *My Guitar Gently Weeps,* over and over again. Third, you conjure up painful memories of your lost love, and then, believe me, it's as if you were Romeo in the flesh, every single note of Eric Clapton's plaintive solo in *While My Guitar Gently Weeps* plunging like a knife into your bleeding heart. And as long as you stay raw and committed, every single time you play that song, no matter where you are, you will be immediately triggered into a tortured state of mind. Strangely, I had never indulged in this type of sadomasochism with the songs of my Chilean childhood. I was way too busy surviving and being a wild child in the playgrounds of Europe to feel sorry for myself. But now, this existential rite of passage into the uncharted land of adolescence opened up the gates of self-awareness and alienation.

I was fourteen, and all I knew was that my first year in high school had been the best year of my life, what with parties and slow dancing, furtive kisses, Halloween in Georgetown, the Redskins against the Cowboys, the Rolling Stones and AC/DC in concert and my brand-new electric guitar and a Peavy 40 amplifier. I'd spend hours with my index finger on the record button, waiting for the right song on the radio to make cheap mix tapes for my friends. Why in the world would I ever want to leave that? I was *Burning for You,* I was *Upside Down,* I was *Turning Japanese,* I was *Back in Black,* I was *In the Air Tonight,* I was *Tainted Love* and I was *Under Pressure.* I was fourteen, obnoxious and totally self-absorbed. At the same time, I didn't really belong anywhere. I went to a French school, but I wasn't French, I had a Chilean passport, but I had spent most of my life away from Chile. I liked Metallica, but I wasn't into speed metal. I wasn't afraid of wearing yellow, and I matched the color of my sweater to my socks, but I wasn't preppy. Sometimes I wore eyeliner, and I was the first one in my school to get an ear pierced, but I wasn't New Wave. I was nothing and I was a bit of everything at the same time. I was the whole of the *The Breakfast Club* wrapped in one enchilada, and that was fine with me. I was fourteen and the rest of the world could go to hell for all I cared . . . except that the dreaded one-year window was coming to an end. Our rental contract was set to expire in July 1982, and we still did not have a visa to move to Mexico.

During that year, my mother had found meaningful work as a social worker with the recently created Family Place, an organization in the once gritty Adams Morgan neighborhood of Washington, DC, mainly supporting the fast-growing Salvadorian community that had fled its war-torn country in the 1980s. My mother had been brought up in the Chilean countryside. The fact that so many from this immigrant community were unpretentious, salt-of-the-earth people made her feel at home. For the first time since we left Chile, I could sense that my mother was genuinely happy. It's fair to say that she hated the idea of leaving again, and so she did what she had to do to stop the move to Mexico.

Many years later, she confessed she used an old trick her grandmother had taught her: she took a small rag and tied it in a knot, then every night, when no one could hear her, she relentlessly beat and beat the knot against a hard edge of the bathroom counter to conjure the spirit of Pontius Pilate with this precise incantation: "*Pilato, Pilato, si no haces lo que te pido, no te desato.*" "Pilate, Pilate, if you don't do what I ask, I won't untie you." Caught in a painful knot, the suffering spirit had no other choice but to obey.

While my mother was chanting, the editor of *Proceso* who had promised my father a Mexican work visa published a series of articles exposing the corruption at Pemex, the state-controlled oil company, which brought down the wrath of the president of Mexico. All political favors were canceled for Julio Scherer, and my father's visa was off the table. When we received the news, my mother breathed a sigh of relief, untied the knot and freed the trapped spirit of Pontius Pilate.

As one door closes, another opens. This particular door had three singular initials engraved on it: I.N.S. That was the Immigration and Naturalization Service, better known as *La Migra* to most of our undocumented Latino brothers and sisters. To us, it meant trying to quickly figure out our legal immigration status. My father was still refusing to apply for political refugee status, so our friend and immigration lawyer Michael Maggio helped him petition for the EB-1 Visa, commonly known as the "Einstein Visa," reserved for individuals who were highly acclaimed in their fields. This meant that while the petition was being processed, which could take years, my father was allowed to work, but my mother could not. Complicating matters further, we were literally stuck inside the continental boundaries of the United States; if we left the country, we would lose our temporary legal immigration status and not be readmitted. I was now happily trapped with no escape in sight, while my parents were now faced with one of the most serious dilemmas any immigrant faces at some point in their journey: to buy or not to buy a house?

During the previous eight years of our exile, our little bungalow house in Santiago, miraculously spared by the military, had been occupied by my mother's younger sister Ana María, her husband and their children I had never met. Back in France, in 1976, as the clock was ticking on our French visa and my father had not yet found a job that could sustain us in any way, shape or form, my parents entertained the idea of selling our little bungalow in Chile to make ends meet. To their surprise, they were asked by the leadership of the resistance in exile not to do so because it was being used as a safehouse for clandestine operations against the dictatorship with an army of stylists creating fake identities of members of the resistence who had entered Chile illegally. My parents relented, now that we were stuck in limbo in the United States, my parents decided to finally sell it. With no

clear path forward other than to follow our blind trust that everything would work out in the end, we bought a split-level brick
house in Bethesda, Maryland, that we could not afford. My bedroom, in the basement, was where I took refuge amid giant
posters of Led Zeppelin, Pink Floyd, Jim Morrison and the
rock/pop collages cut out from the pages of *Creem* magazine.

Our situation, viewed from the prism of a responsible adult,
was of course, completely unsustainable. My father was now a self-
employed writer with a nebulous immigration status and a hefty
mortgage. He had to hustle a living every way possible because he
was the only legal bread winner in the family. I vividly remember
the toll that this burden took on him. Oftentimes I would walk into
his small study, the floor literally littered with dozens of crunched
up pages, a cemetery of half starts, to ask him something, and he
would either say, "Not now" or, if he wasn't totally possessed in the
moment, he would stop typing and turn to me, his fingers suspended in mid-air, half of them bandaged, the others dried up,
about to crack and bleed from the stress and the intensity it took to
type on a mechanical typewriter for twelve hours a day.

By Spring 1983, when the time came for all of us to show up
again at the I.N.S. in Baltimore for our yearly "check in" and petition for a Green Card, my father and Mike Maggio came up with
a bold and daring idea. At our interview, my father calmly sat
down in front of the agent and said, "We want the US government
to deport us." According to immigration law, at the time, expelled
immigrants had to be deported back to their country of origin.

"The only problem," my father continued, "is that the Chilean
government will not allow me to go back. So, if you could please
request the State Department to intervene and ask them to allow
us to return, we will happily self-deport."

"But I thought you were applying for a Green Card. Why do
you want us to deport you? No one has ever made this type of
request," said the agent, the same incredulous look on his face as
the customs officer at the end of the pier in Baltimore. "Ever!"

"It's very simple. If you can't give my clients a Green Card," answered our lawyer, "then we demand the US Government do everything in its power to deport them back to Chile. Now, if you want to save yourself the trouble of convincing the Chilean government to take them back, then my clients will drop their self-deportation request and in return accept your generous offer of a Green Card."

The agent paused, blinked and barely contained an exasperated sigh. "If you will excuse me for a moment," he said and then exited the room.

The moment turned into hours. The agent finally came back, sat down and said with a deadpan voice, "You have been approved for a Green Card."

I thought, "Yes! It's all finally coming together."

When my parents bought the new house the year before, they bet on the future as they always do and bought me a brand-new, queen-size bed for my fifteenth birthday. I thought I had died and gone to heaven. A simple bed, my bed, something that most kids take for granted, was proof that I finally belonged in this world. I had found a safe place to rest and gaze up at the ceiling, listening to the Doors and the screaming howl of Jim Morrison's insolent voice. It was, of course, an illusion, but a necessary illusion. It was almost as if the universe knew that I needed that momentary pause in order to gather my strengths and feel what it was like to safely hold the world in the palm of my hand before having it inevitably taken away from me again.

Indeed, nothing lasts forever. Just when I had fallen asleep in my basement wrapped in my dreams of sweet belonging, my father rushed down the stairs and woke me up late on the night of August 22, 1983, his face glowing in the dark, tears of joy in his eyes, his arms holding me tight.

"Rodrigo, they let me back. We're going back."

Two weeks later, we were on a plane to Santiago. And just like that, exile was over.

Or so I thought.

BOOK II
SONGS OF RETURN

Don't be satisfied with stories.
How things have gone with others.
Unfold your own myth.

Rumi

AN IMAGINARY RETURN
(On the Plane, 1983)

Every documentary
Every image
Of a return to Chile from exile
Has a long shot of the Andes
La Cordillera
Viewed through the small egg-shaped window of the plane
As it makes its slow descent
Into Santiago

As a filmmaker
I pay attention to details
I notice the camera doing its best to avoid
The slight diffusion
Around the worn edges of the window frame
The inevitable scratched pane
Technically called
A "bleed hole"

I settle on the eyes of our protagonist
Soft
A thin veil of sadness reflects the bright blue skies
Outside
I imagine

That he welcomes the distancing effect of the camera crew
Like I welcome words on a page
We create these filters to help us manage
Our pain
We know we need to be clearheaded
Present
We can't afford to break down the dam

Later
Much later
I imagine
After the plane lands
And he goes through the obligatory passport control
Answers an endless stream of questions
And the luggage carousel goes
Round and round
He stretches his whole body on the tip of his toes
To catch a glimpse of his family and friends
Waiting for his return
Out beyond
The plexiglass doors
Anxiously waving hand-written signs
Hoisting children up on their shoulders
Children he has only seen in photographs
And after the automatic doors slide open
The hurried walk that turns into a run
The open arms
The first embrace that seems to last
An eternity
Nobody wants to let him go
The car ride
Blurred memories zooming by
The *empanadas*
The *ensalada a la chilena*
The smell of sliced tomatoes

And the obligatory *vino tinto*
The old songs
The memory of those who didn't make it
The awkward silences
The cold night without central heating
The bed in the soothing darkness
And after all this
Maybe
Just maybe
Our protagonist imagines he can finally
Let go
Allow himself to feel the moment
Without having to pinch
the soft underside of his forearm
and be reminded that he is truly
most definitively
Here
That this is not a dream.
That everything that happened
Happened
That there is no return
That he has come from the future
To bury the past
Maybe
Just maybe.

I turn to look at my father. He is lost in thought, looking down at the *cordillera* below with its rising peaks and cutting crests, the subject of a thousand and one odes and poems. He takes one last glimpse before it fades into the mountains of the upcoming Central Valley. Maybe he sees a scar? Armor? A dragon's tail? I try to remember it as the same *cordillera* I used to draw as a child when it meant nothing more, nothing less than a few geometrical patterns on a piece of paper, a simple reflection of what I saw back then, when I lifted my little eyes and looked at the sky for inspiration before I knew the meaning of distance.

Where is that inspiration now? It still must be there, somewhere, living, breathing in Chile. It must be. I've carried the original musical score deep inside in my castle for all these years and now all I have to do is find the corresponding song, somewhere, somehow and everything will be all right.

The captain speaks, the wheels come down, squeaking beneath the fuselage. The plane lands and, for lack of my stuffed rabbit lost a long time ago in a hotel room in Rome, I'm holding on to my racing heart as if my life depends on it. We walk down the metal staircase into the cold air of an early September morning, 1983, Santiago, Chile.

I take my first steps on the tarmac. Everything after that is a blur. Some things are better left to the imagination.

THE SMOG OF THE DRAGON
(Chile, 1983)

Our little bungalow house where I grew up was gone, my grandparents' idyllic two-story stone house in Providencia razed to the ground to make way for an apartment building, my old school relocated and the sunny Andes of my childhood drawings all but disappeared into a thick toxic haze descending like some evil curse or the lingering breath of a dragon. The smog in Santiago was like the haunting voice of Pinochet on the evening news, announcing the return of the dreaded *toque de queda*, the nightly curfew, and the deployment of 18,000 soldiers on the streets of Chile. His voice was pervasive, invasive and poisonous. It was everywhere. If Pinochet had robbed us of our freedoms, then the smog had robbed us of our mountain chain, our national symbol of permanence and intimacy. If I had looked a little deeper, I would have recognized in this absence one of the most fundamental experiences of exile, that feeling of dislocation and suspension, but I had not returned home to look for exile.

The smog was more than just a popular metaphor turning Santiago into a fairytale with dragons and evil curses; it was also the industrial byproduct of an accelerated economic boom, the famous "Chilean Miracle." This boom, fueled in part by a generous flow of foreign investments after the coup, cheap imports and the easy availability of credit, gave rise to a new standard of living for millions of middle-class Chileans who had welcomed the military coup, if not with open arms, at the very least with a sigh of relief. When we arrived, a recession was wreaking havoc with the Chilean economy. It was one thing to hear the news from afar of this economic model imposed on Chile, another to see with my own eyes what it had done to the country I had dreamt of. The misery was everywhere as I cautiously ventured into the streets of Santiago and explored the *caracoles*, those wretched low-rent mini-malls shaped like snail shells, cheap facsimiles of Frank Lloyd Wright's design of the Guggenheim, that had started to sprout everywhere in Santiago in the late 70s, attracting every small business imaginable. Those businesses were now dying, sprouting closing sale signs on every spiraling floor.

I noticed a man sweeping the sidewalk from one end to the other. He would pause, light a cigarette, take a few puffs, then start sweeping again, or rather pushing the dirt back the other way. Incredulous, I asked him for a light for my cigarette and got him to explain to me what he was doing. He was a member of POJH (Occupational Program for Heads of Household), a government employment program created to mitigate the effects of a 20% rate of unemployment (up to 50% in the small towns) and give heads of household something to do in exchange for less than the minimum wage. One-hundred thousand people were put to work, painting over political graffiti, digging holes and then filling them back up, and endlessly sweeping the streets and plazas of Santiago.

"What else are we supposed to do?" he sighed, asking me for one of my American cigarettes. "People are eating cats and dogs. . . . And right here in Providencia, I saw a doctor selling goat cheese from door to door to make ends meet."

This was not the deal the majority of the Chilean people who supported the coup had made with themselves or with the military regime. They wanted progress and economic stability, even if it meant in exchange turning a blind eye to the Chilean nightmare of state-sponsored terrorism. In the collective dreams and imported desires of the Chilean people, filled with televisions, refrigerators, washing machines, blenders, cars and every other imported good under the sun, materialism was now associated with peace, prosperity and the strong fatherly figure of General Pinochet. In his speech celebrating the triumph of the (rigged) 1980 constitution and his election as "President," Pinochet promised that one in seven Chileans would soon own a car and that one in five Chileans would own a television. The past, *my* past, was now literally black and white—as opposed to the color TVs to be imported—and forever associated with Salvador Allende, empty pots and the chaos of a failed revolution. It was a perfectly understandable human choice. The last time Chileans tried to ignore the tyranny of false binary choices and find a third way out of that dark cell of history, they were beaten, tortured and murdered with impunity.

In casual conversations, my Chilean family called it *ponerse la corbata*, putting on a suit and tie. Besides choosing to survive and burn their favorite books and records and bury them alongside their ideals, many supporters of the revolution were forced to alter their physical appearance. If they ever wanted a job again in this *Nuevo* Chile, if they ever wanted to feed their children and survive the long winters to come, they were going to have to cut their hair, shave their beards, put on a suit and tie and bow their heads into submission. In other words, like children forced to go to school, they became complicit collaborators in their own oppression. As a society, how do you then channel the energy required to sustain the toll of such moral dissonance? How do you make a nation living inside of a horror movie believe they are instead actors in a sentimental feel-good movie with a happy ending? How do you make the dead disappear in the mind's eye? Among other tactics, you create the Chilean Telethon.

Borrowing from the Jerry Lewis playbook, the now famous Mario Kreutzberger, a.k.a. Don Francisco, host of the legendary *Sábado Gigante* (Gigantic Saturday), the longest running TV show in Spanish-language television, brought together every censorship-approved entertainer, every radio and TV station, every corporate sponsor imaginable to produce a twenty-seven-hour-long televised national spectacle he dubbed "Crusade of Love." The goal was to raise one million dollars to fund rehabilitation facilities for disabled children. The year was 1978, the same year of the advent of color television across Chile and of the imposition of Military Decree 291, better known as the Law of Amnesty that exonerated any member of the Chilean government of any crime, be it political or criminal in nature, committed since the coup of September 11, 1973. There would be no public recognition of the thousands of tortured and murdered bodies scattered across Chile, even after the shocking news of the discovery of the remains of fifteen *desaparecidos*, the disappeared, hidden in an abandoned mine in Lonquén, thirty miles from Santiago. Instead of facing this perverse complicity, Chileans could watch the mangled, crippled and broken bodies of innocent children crawling on prosthetic legs and walking on crutches with big puppy-sad eyes staring back at them in the darkness of their living rooms.

"What was mobilized there," according to my friend Marcial Godoy of the Hemispheric Institute in New York, and still remains present to this day on Chilean television as a key mechanism of social control, "is the political instrumentalization of *lástima*, of pity. This allows for a displacement onto others, in this case disabled children, all the emotional trauma generated by the dictatorship, the sorrow, the fear and the affect, through the idiom of pity."

In 1983, I could sense this perverse atmosphere in every look, every small exchange around me. This was not a language I recognized. This third-rate imitation of American capitalism, this gray, poisoned Chile beaten to submission in parts, this Chile governed not only by fear and terror but also by the seduction of consumerism; this Chile I did not recognize, nor did I want to recognize it.

And yet, in that moment of crisis, with the return of thousands of exiles, with an economy in recession and a middle class

waking up for the first time to its broken dreams, driven to finally find the courage to protest in public, the future seemed wide
open. Once I started to look beyond my desire for a picture-perfect postcard of the *cordillera*, I started experiencing how
Chileans were resisting the military dictatorship, I began to feel
the resonance of something familiar with my country.

On September 11, 1983, ten years after the coup, my father
and I exited the Metro station near the Moneda Presidential
Palace to the sound of shrieking sirens, tear gas burning our eyes
and the chaos of bodies running toward us escaping the white
sticks swinging behind them wielded by members of the fascist
Patria y Libertad paramilitary brigades. The brigades had been
given free rein to crack our skulls during those early days of
protests.

"*¡Corre!*" shouted my father, and we took off down the
Alameda, together with hundreds of other protesters, zigzagging
between food carts, kiosks and street vendors. We joined other
waves of protesters who had found a safe space to jump up and
down and shout, "*¡El que no salta es Pinochet! ¡El que no salta
es Pinochet!*" The one who doesn't jump is Pinochet!

Dissent, humor, creativity and aerobics, Chilean protests had
it all, as they still do today.

I couldn't believe it! The songs of my childhood were ringing out right there in front of me, out in the open, for all to hear,
all to sing and shout to the heavens. You could still get killed or
beaten up for singing them, but at least the fear seemed to be
gone. My joy and disbelief were interrupted by a long olive-green
bus disgorging cops in riot gear swinging their batons at anything
that moved. As they descended on us, everyone scattered again
only to be blocked by the *guanaco*, a tank spitting water with
pressures strong enough to knock us off our feet, or sprayed by
the *zorrillo*, a small armored car that gassed us at close range, in-
ducing vomiting and painful bronchial damage.

I was sixteen and immortal, and there was nothing like the
adrenaline rush conjured up by being in the middle of a righteous

riot. There is no doubt that one of the reasons I would come back to live in Chile, two years later, in 1985 after graduating from high school other than the desire to feed my survivor's guilt with punishment, was to relive the intensity of that first encounter. I wanted to experience again that feeling of recognition you see in a stranger's eyes when you're jumping up and down together for joy and then you're running next to each other, a hair away from being smashed by a rubber club or taken into the police van and having the shit kicked out of you.

Yes, I was immortal and stupid, but the only thing that mattered was that I could finally recognize Chile in the rebellious eyes of a woman I had never met before who handed me a slice of lemon to chew on to calm the burning effects of tear gas, her voice reassuring me that we were going to be all right. I saw the spirit of Chilean resistance in the sounds of a thousand pots banging in unison in the night, defying with their cacophony the very existence of a curfew. I felt it in the madness of my uncles and aunts running around their house waiting for the designated hour to turn on all their appliances; vacuum cleaners, blenders, washing machines—with the insane hope that if everybody did it at once, it would overwhelm the electrical grid and create a brown out. It was absurd sabotage in a pre-internet age of communication. It never worked, but no matter, the idea was to make Chile ungovernable, and we were not going to rest until Pinochet, like the dragon at the end of a fairy tale, left and never came back.

Standing in the eye of this hurricane, one of the guiding lights of this resistance was the Vicaría de la Solidaridad, an organization created by the Chilean Catholic Church in response to the need to denounce and document the human rights abuses happening in Chile, with the hope that one day when democracy returned to this land, there would be a sense of accountability and a way to hear, honor and recognize out in the open and in a court of law the voices of those who had been abused by the dictatorship. The offices of the Vicaría were attached to the Cathedral of Santiago and enjoyed the full protection of the Church, an institution that even the military could not mess with. Queno Ahumanda, one of my father's oldest friends, worked at the Vicaría and invited us to visit and meet with the organization of relatives of the *detenidos desaparecidos*, those who had been disappeared, the dissidents deemed enemies of the state who had been detained by the authorities only to never be seen again. Their relatives were left to live in a cruel, suspended state of uncertainty.

Holding black and white photographs of their loved ones, they would demand to know, "Where are they? Are they dead? Are they still alive? Where are their bodies?" Organized and made up mostly of fearless women, they dared to chain themselves day after day to the gates of the Palace of Justice, suffering beatings and imprisonment in order to relentlessly demand justice for their loved ones. In so doing, they were creating some of the most iconic images of resistance of the late twentieth century.

We all sat down in a circle, and they began to tell us their stories. One victim, Viviana Díaz, described how her father Víctor Díaz was sleeping in a small room in a safe house where he had been hiding for three years under an assumed identity, when the secret police came for him. Once they identified him, they started torturing him for information in his living room. When nothing came of it, they took him away in his pajamas. He was fifty-six at the time. Viviana never saw her father again. It would take her another decade to finally find out that he had been murdered after spending one year in various torture centers. The security forces had wrapped his body in a burlap sack, tied it to metal rails and loaded him onto a helicopter that flew out to sea, where they tossed his body.

Story after story, there was something about the tender dignity, the stone-cold anger of their voices, something about their *testimonios* that transcended any experience of loss I had ever experienced before. Their voices poured into my being, flooding into every corner I had safely hidden away from the world.

And something else happened, and this I realized much later. They also washed and cleansed my childhood songs from the self-pitying darkness I had relegated them to. Beyond a deep sense of sadness that will never leave me, I am grateful for the gift these women gave me that day. They taught me how to bear witness, an invaluable lesson for my later years as a documentary film-maker. They taught me how to be present with enough empathy and humility to honor their open wounds while listening with just enough distance not to be overwhelmed by my own emotions. I remember making a conscious decision in that moment that I would not call my father *padre* or the affectionate *papi* in their presence. I could feel the weight of their tragedy and I was mindful of the privilege of having my father alive next to me, while they were missing their own parents. I didn't want my words to remind them of their loss. Was it out of shame of having survived? All I knew back then, back in that room filled with the kind of heartbreak that made my exile look like a picnic, was that I needed to call my father by his name. And so, I did. I called him Ariel and, for the first time, I felt like an adult. For the first time, I felt at peace being neither here nor there. The truth is that after that day in Chile, it took me thirty years to call him "father" again.

It rained on the morning of my last day in Santiago. The smog cleared just enough to let the missing *cordillera* momentarily sparkle through the vanishing haze and announce to anyone that cared that it was still there. I looked up at the skies and closed my eyes. I knew every moment must come to an end, and yet, we stubbornly wished to hang on to it. I was starving for a country to belong to, and those first returns were like sitting down in front of a banquet. It didn't matter that Chile was still a dictatorship and in a state of war with itself, contaminated by political ideology and violence. During our ten years away, family members had died, new ones were born, everything had changed, but it didn't matter; I plunged into it and ate it all up, the good and the bad, because I wanted to belong there so desperately. And I kept going back, again and again, living as if it was my last night on earth.

THE PINOCHET BOYS
(USA, Chile, 1985)

I was eighteen and a senior at my French high school. I was ready to leave behind boring Bethesda, speaking English and a country of bozos who had elected Ronald Reagan to a second term. I was so impatient to leave it all behind that I even got myself kicked out of school three months before graduation. It was the grand finale of my long history of disciplinary tribulations in the French educational system. It didn't help that my first return to Chile, in 1983, had unfortunately placed me outside the everyday experiences of most of my friends and ripped apart any semblance of belonging or assimilation I had created for myself during those past five years in the quiet suburb of Bethesda, Maryland.

I was ready for another escape.

When I landed again in Chile in 1985, after finally being allowed to graduate from high school, the country was slowly coming out of its recession. But it was too late to calm down the anger and the unrest that swept the nation. I arrived in Santiago in time for another September 11 wave of protests. The opposition was now divided into two camps: those who wanted to defeat Pinochet through an armed insurrection, with 700 terrorist bombings in 1984 alone, and those who believed in a non-violent resistance against the dictatorship. Amazingly enough, the epic biopic *Gandhi*, starring Ben Kingsley, had an incalculable impact on the hearts and minds of Chileans and, in many ways, on the future of Chilean democracy. Censorship in Chile was randomly applied the way a dog owner can give his dog just enough leash to smell the flowers and then yank it back, choking it at a moment's notice. For example, Andre Wajda's overtly political film *Danton*, about the Reign of Terror during the French Revolution, was allowed to be screened, but Terry Gilliam's *Brazil*, an irreverent take on Orwell's *1984*, was forbidden. I remember sneaking into a mall in Santiago, after midnight, with my uncle, the documentary filmmaker Nacho Agüero, to view a secret screening of *Brazil* on a small screen. But *Gandhi* had inexplicably escaped the strict control of the military censors and was released in 1983 to rave reviews and sold-out showings for over a year. At the time, movie theaters were one of the few places people could publicly express their political opinions without the fear of being violently repressed, even if it meant shouting in the dark. Loud clapping accompanied the singing of lyrics such as "*Y va a caer, y se va acabar, la dictadura militar*" (And he will fall, and it will end, the military dictatorship) every single time the lights went down or if the projectionist was running late. I saw *Gandhi* a couple of times in Santiago because every screening turned into a political carnival. Audiences would give Ben Kinsgley standing ovations throughout the entire three-hour epic as they claimed this momentary safe space in a sea of indiscriminate violence. Gandhi, for all his faults as an individual and as a historical figure, had the power to inspire and embolden a whole generation of young Chilean activists thirsty for a peaceful way to reclaim and regain their freedoms.

I could see it everywhere. The young had stopped being afraid, while the old were planning out how to politically unite a fractured center-left opposition and defeat Pinochet's plebiscite slated for 1988 behind the scenes. It would be a simple yes or no answer. A "yes" meant another eight years of "President" Pinochet; a "no" meant elections the following year for a new president along with members of a newly created senate and chamber of deputies.

Meanwhile, the military was given *carte blanche* to repress the population. Soldiers were using live ammunition in the shantytowns, and a newly formed death squad, calling itself *Ghurkas* because of the singular shape of the Nepalese knives used to cut the throats of their victims, had recently kidnapped José Manuel Parada, a human rights activist, just as he was picking up his children from school in broad daylight. They dumped his body in a ditch near the airport a few days later alongside two other activists. Their throats had been slit. The military, sensing its power slipping away, had seemingly decided to go back to the random terror tactics of the early days of dictatorship.

I chose to ignore the warning signs and plunged right into the eye of the storm without a thought for my mother as she waved goodbye to me at the airport in the United States in 1985. After all, I had gone back to Chile to feel what it was like to live under a fascist dictatorship and, in the process, punish myself to make up for those ten years of absence during my Golden Exile.

My plan was simple. I would go to Chile and live with my aunt until I heard back from the University of California, Berkeley, the only university I had applied to—just to keep things as straightforward and as dangerously precarious as possible. I had asked for a Spring 1986 admission. If I got in, I would go to college in the good old USA. If I didn't, I would give up my Green Card, stay in Chile and, like every other eighteen-year-old living under Pinochet, try to figure out what to do with the rest of my life. It sounded like a good plan to me and, to my parents' credit, not once did they say, "That sounds kind of reckless, Rodrigo."

By the time I went back to Chile, my parents and my little brother had moved to Durham, North Carolina, where my father had gotten a three-year contract at Duke University to teach only one semester but spend the rest of the year living and writing in Chile. He planned to drag my six-year-old brother across the hemisphere, the seasons and various school systems. If that sounded a little crazy, it was, but that had become our family tradition.

After arriving in Santiago, I was soon running for my life, bullets flying, tear gas canisters crashing around me. Strapped to my shoulders was a thirty-pound portable audio deck attached via cable to a Sony Betacam camera in the hands of my friend Yerko Yankovic, one of the videographers of *Teleanálisis*, the only independent Chilean video news agency operating both inside and outside the law. Chile's strict censors did not just control films like *Brazil*, they also had their hands on everything from book publishing to public art, radio and especially television. After the coup, the military had executed a systematic campaign to destroy the cultural legacy of the Chilean Revolution by painting over thousands of murals, burning all the television video archives, educational materials, magazines and books they could get their hands on. Even the *charango*, a type of small guitar, had been forbidden! And more ominously for us, on the very first day of the coup in 1973, the third edition of my father's book *How to Read Donald Duck,* sitting at the printers in the port city of Valparaiso ready to be shipped, was immediately seized and thrown into the sea, making the first two editions that type of rare book that fetches thousands on eBay today.

Cultural resistance to the dictatorship became not just an essential tool to express one's personal demons unleashed by the stress of being young and living under the heavy boot of a military dictatorship, but also a communal space where Chileans could create an alternative popular history that could get them through that long night of fascism. By 1985, *Teleanálisis* was one of the central engines of this cultural resistance. Every month, *Teleanálisis* produced an hour-long program made up of three or four short segments documenting a reality that was otherwise absent from the mainstream media: soup kitchens, women as community organizers, the challenges of non-violent resistance, student activism, breakdancing as means for peaceful conflict resolution, Chilean rock 'n' roll and the emergence of an under-

ground culture openly contemptuous of political parties and ide-
ologies. It was an amazing time to be young and rebellious.

While violently repressing with one hand, Pinochet started
relaxing his grip on some aspects of this nascent youth culture
with the other. He even went on television and declared with his
infamous, nauseating nasal tone that Chile was no longer a hard
dictatorship but a "dicta-blanda" (a soft dictatorship). This meant
that as long as the youth of Chile stayed out of political organiz-
ing and street protests, the security forces would turn a relatively
blind eye and let them dance and drink the night away. This, of
course, did not apply to the LGBTQ community, which had always been savagely repressed no matter who was in charge.

One of the centers of this counterculture was an old rehabil-
itated warehouse belonging to the syndicate of Santiago's retired
trolley conductors. Dubbed "El Trolley," it became one of the
epicenters of experimental theatre, dance, film, music and performance. One of the founders of this space, playwright and director Ramón Griffero, who had studied theatre while in exile in
Brussels, once described to me the first time the secret police
showed up at the Trolley, expecting the typical political subver-
sive stereotype: long hair, ponchos, acoustic guitars, stern sad
faces, fists raised in the air. Instead, they came face to face with
a punk band called the *Pinochet Boys* and a mosh pit of drunken
euphoric kids.

"Yes, they're the *Pinochet Boys*," Ramón told the utterly confused military agents, who simply could not comprehend the concept of irony.

They had landed on another planet, a parallel universe divorced from the political pamphlets and folkloric postcards of a
Chile frozen in time before the military coup. It was a past these
Chilean youths knew nothing about anyway, since they had been
brought up without any sort of functional or institutional collective memory of life before fascism. Pinochet was all they knew.

There were other bands with cryptic names — *Los Prisioneros*
(the Prisoners), *Los Electrodomésticos* (The Home Appliances),

La Banda del Pequeño Vicio (The Little Vice Band)—all of them dismissing the polarizing dogmas of the twentieth century, dogmas that after all were directly responsible for the failure of the revolution and the subsequent military coup. Tired of being the victims of history in a classic Generation X fashion they had decided to remove themselves from it and in the process piss everyone off, left and right, and find a new language to move forward into the future without asking anyone's permission.

Back in 1983, much to the chagrin of my parents, I had gone down to Georgetown's famous Commander Salamander store in Washington DC, and gotten my left ear pierced to wear a little diamond-like stud earring that I refused to take out before returning to Chile on that first trip back.

"Why are you always provoking people like that?" my mother chastised me as we were packing our suitcases.

In 1983, Chile was still a deeply conservative and Catholic society. With fascism in power, rampant homophobia, sexism and a sense of cultural and geographical isolation breeding the worst aspects of provinciality, of course my earring was not appreciated by most of the older Chileans I met. The counterculture of 1985 had not yet reached Chile, so apparently only those relegated to the distant margins of society, such as gays, transsexuals and petty criminals wore an earring. But I looked like a clean-cut, upper-class kid—light brown hair, green eyes, no discernable indigenous features. It made no sense to anyone. I was basically begging for a beating.

I remember accompanying my father to a secret meeting—all meetings were secret back then—with the editorial staff of an opposition magazine. I couldn't help but notice the uneasy glances. Later, when the meeting was over and we were rushing back home to beat the curfew, my father scolded me for not removing my earring. I had apparently offended them in some way. What a load of shit, I thought at the time. What a bunch of *viejos vinagres*, old curmudgeons, sold out baby boomers. And they were to be the architects of a future democracy after Pinochet? I knew that they had been thrown in jail, beaten, persecuted—that they were courageous men full of good intentions, but still, their generational reaction left a bad taste in my mouth.

If today I had to put my finger on one of the key moments that sealed my fate, and possibly the fate of my country, it would be that one: when a group of baby boomers, haunted by their mistakes and their fears of repeating the past, did not actually recognize my generation for who we were for the youthful liberating knowledge we had brought with us from exile or crested from the margins of society. Any deviation from the norm, any offense, any discomfort was a danger to the negotiated transition they were planning with the military and the center, more conservative Christian Democrats. I should have known right then and there that no matter the outcome of Chile's political future, the young and the defiant would bear the real brunt of the impending political transition. Children always wind up paying for their parents' mistakes, don't they?

But back in 1985, diving in and out of the Chilean underground like a butterfly, flirting with belonging, not quite sure where to land, the future seemed irrelevant. I was completely enthralled with my work as a production assistant at *Teleanálisis* and the program's holistic approach to cultural resistance. The videographers and reporters were working with foreign press passes given to them by mostly European media outlets in exchange for footage they could not obtain under other circumstances. The one-hour video documentaries were "officially" created for foreign consumption and were often smuggled out of the country in diplomatic attaché cases of governments friendly to the Chilean resistance. In order to create plausible deniability, every tape started with a clear notice in bold type: "Any public screening of this material is forbidden in Chile." That was a subterfuge, of course, because the main purpose of those videos, beyond educating the world about the Chilean resistance and solidifying Pinochet's isolation as an international pariah, was to make hundreds of copies and distribute them underground across Chile.

I remember loading up a non-descript van with a TV set and a Betamax player and driving to a shanty town, sneaking under the very noses of the police and the military. We would usually set up a screening room in the main hall of a church, because it was safe. Hundreds of people would come and gather around the small television set and watch uncensored news and forbidden images about their lives, their dreams and their everyday struggles. They could not see themselves represented anywhere else on Chilean media, but right there, for an hour, huddled together inside that church, in defiance of the censorship laws of the Chilean state, they could see themselves as protagonists of their own lives. The documentaries would then elicit public conversations about civil society in ways that would have been impossible anywhere else, nurturing the kind of public discourse necessary to rebuild a future democracy. I would sit by the Betamax during the screenings and observe while the audience watched those video depictions so close to their own lives. I will never forget the feeling of seeing everyday people recognize themselves in those videos. This is what I want to do, I told myself. This is where I want to be.

In that collective space of resistance, I could feel a palpable sense of immediacy and urgency, which decades later would form the emotional and aesthetic blueprint of my present life as a community-centered documentary filmmaker.

Meanwhile, the path of my life was as good as the flip of a coin. In November, I received an acceptance letter from the University of California, Berkeley to start as a freshman in the Spring of 1986. Fate had knocked again, and I opened the door, as I always do.

I was nineteen and, just when I thought I had found myself, it was time to get lost again.

COLLEGE FRAGMENTS
(Berkeley, California and
Durham, North Carolina, 1986-1989)

I landed in Berkeley on a cold January night in 1986 with a single suitcase, ready to dive deep into English, my third language, and experience the intellectual thrills of American academia. The first thing I bought myself was a Roget's *Thesaurus*. Next was a used Smith Corona Coronet Chronomantic Super 12 electric typewriter with a detachable white-out cartridge. Third was a used checkered jacket in the ska style. Last but not least was an Alien Sex Fiend T-shirt. I had never heard of the band, but I liked the name.

I loved everything about Berkeley: getting stoned in People's Park, eating pizza at Fat Slice on Telegraph Avenue, laughing with street comedian Stoney Burke, tripping with the Bubble Lady, unauthorized midnight candlelight concerts at the Greek Theater with local street musicians, sneaking jugs of $2.50 Gallo wine into the Berkeley Rep movie theatre where Werner Herzog ate his shoe in order to see Fellini's *Satyricon*, buying used books at Cody's, arguing about Derrida and Kierkegaard and aesthetics and Antonioni with my new American friends at Café Roma, skipping class on a fresh sunny afternoon, breaking into the Pacific Film Archives to look for a copy of Jodorowsky's cult classic *El Topo*, dancing at La Peña Cultural Center, throwing eggs at Vice President George Bush's motorcade with Crazy Horse and the Communist Youth League, running the CIA recruiters off campus, watching the ROTC building burn to the ground and the infamous Barrington Hall wine parties, where we danced the night away in a tribal haze of sweat and psychedelics.

Memory has a way of smoothing the rough edges of our past experiences and, yes, it is easy to forget the darker, more depressing side of Berkeley and the Bay Area when conjuring up the greatest hits from the eighties. Homelessness was rampant, and sometimes, when it was cold, rainy and gray, you could feel the impact of Reagan's repeal of the Mental Health Systems Act in 1981, which led to the closing of hundreds of clinics around the country with thousands of unmedicated patients literally thrown into the streets to fend for themselves. And even further in the shadows, the same CIA that had helped destroy Chile's democracy was now systematically spreading crack cocaine in poor urban areas, feeding black and brown bodies into prison cells.

After a few months, I wound up sharing a cavernous studio space with three other Berkeley students. It was located in one of the first industrial warehouses turned into living apartments in Emeryville, a small city of 4,000 inhabitants squeezed between Berkeley and Oakland and bordered by the East Bay. This was years before gentrification brought in such businesses as IKEA and Pixar Studios to that gritty industrial town where gambling was legal (when it wasn't anywhere else in California) and the sheriff was named Cain. There were train tracks right at the back of our warehouse, where the conductors would regularly park their engines during their lunch break, walk up to the Black and White liquor store on San Pablo and get a fifth of cheap gin wrapped in a paper bag.

I'd never had American friends. There was Scott Sampler, who studied Art History and Philosophy and is now a wine maker in the Central Coast of California; Neal Michaelis, who studied Art and wound-up making paragliding documentaries in Nepal; and Greg Hittelman, whose ancestors, like mine, were also from Odessa and who studied English and is now working in communications with organizations that follow the dirty money connected to African arms dealers and war profiteers. We had plenty in common. Of course, we loved Antonioni, early Pink Floyd, *Don Giovanni* and a wide array of Dada cultural products. But there was something else, something deeper. I soon realized that every one of my friends had divorced parents; all three had experienced a broken family in their childhood. Back then, I had never had any close contact with the consequences of divorce. My friends were hesitant to talk about it, but I was curious. I could sense in them this deep undercurrent of loss when they opened up and told me their stories of divided homes and shattered expectations. They had two homes, two parents living their separate lives, and they were stuck in the middle.

"You guys grew up in exile just like me!" I would tell them. "Sure, you're in the same country, speaking the same language, it's different from my experience. But still. . . ." And I would leave my sentence hanging in midair. "Still," I would continue, "you know what it feels like to be torn apart, to lose your home."

I would leave it there because I knew that even if they didn't say it, it was a painful concept for them. For me, this was the first time I was able to relate to Anglo-Americans in a way that made me feel as if they we were together on the same journey of healing and self-discovery. It's fascinating to think that just a few years later, by the time demographers and marketing data analysts started dissecting us, this experience of the loss that comes with divorced parents would be one of the main characteristics of Generation X.

One thing I did not share in common with them was that I had to work twenty hours a week to comply with the terms of my grandparents' college trust fund. I had to pay for my own living expenses. I worked for $4.25 an hour at an ice cream shop on the corner of Telegraph and Bancroft, right across from the main entrance to the university. I would work late nights, by myself, cleaning dozens of twenty-gallon stainless steel containers in a large room with wall-to-wall windows overlooking Telegraph Avenue. Between 10:00 p.m. and 1:00 a.m, I would slide open a small window and play loud classical music so that the homeless could enjoy it along with me. I would swing the two powerful spray jets like an orchestra conductor, while outside on a good night at least ten homeless men would sit on the sidewalk and listen to the concert. I remember one night I came out to smoke a cigarette and was approached by a man who looked like he could have been my father's age. He wanted to thank me for sharing the music with them. He used to have a family, a wife and daughters, a house, a pet, a job and a classical music collection. He had lost it all to drug addiction. He told me his story and started crying after he had nothing left to say. He seemed so helpless in his ragged tweed jacket and his worn wingtips. I hugged him. I had to. And he kept on crying on my shoulder until there was nothing left but an embarrassed silence. I saw him a few more times, standing in the night, motionless, listening to Shubert quartets or Mozart arias mixed with the clanging sounds of the washroom, and then someone told the police about what I was doing, and they ordered my manager to put an end to the concerts for the homeless and obstructing the sidewalk, whereupon I told my manager to go fuck himself.

I could always find another job. The arrival of a Gap store on Telegraph Avenue, the slow creeping gentrification that would explode a decade later, opened up plenty of opportunities to make fancy sandwiches, pour expensive coffees or help sell tie dye T-shirts for tourists looking to get in touch with their inner hippie. Even though it was all around me, screaming from every corner, I chose to ignore the Disneyfication of Berkeley's freewheeling legacy and instead submerged myself and explore the cultural legacy of resistance so central to my imaginary Berkeley experience. I had been there as a toddler in 1968, in pre-literate anarchist rapture, and wanted to see if the spirit of the free-speech movement and Mario Salvo's grainy black and white image urging us to throw our bodies upon the gears and the levers of the machine was still there, living and breathing within me. The answer was yes.

While I was throwing my grain of sand into the Chilean fascist machinery by working at *Teleanálisis* 6,000 miles away, the students at UC Berkeley had been demanding that the regents of the university system divest $3.1 billion dollars from the retirement fund of companies doing business with the South African government. In 1985, the apartheid regime of P. W. Botha had imposed a state of emergency eerily similar to the one in Chile. We were two peoples joined in solidarity by our struggle for liberation and bound by the same steel, rubber bullets and tear gas raining down on our bodies. In the Spring of 1986, a coalition consisting of the United People of Color, the Campaign against Apartheid and the UC Divestment Coalition made our final push for full divestment. The eyes of the nation were on us. Representative Ron Dellums' Anti-Divestment Bill was stuck in Congress, and no one had been able to force a university to divest from South Africa.

In late March, after a rowdy rally that ended with Richie Havens singing his famous rendition of the song "Freedom," we marched on California Hall, the offices of the regents of the California University System, and built fifteen shanties from donated construction materials. They were immediately declared a public hazard. The police tore them down and arrested sixty-one protesters. Thousands of us came back the next day and we marched down to California Hall again. This time we shut it down, literally. I remember the thrill of helping nail two-by-fours onto the ten-foot ornate wooden doors. We built twenty new shanties that day.

I remember wanting to connect all the struggles of resistance I had experienced in my life in that moment. I took a brush and painted, on one of the shanties I had helped build, the word "VENCEREMOS" (We shall overcome), the iconic slogan of the Chilean Revolution my mother had forbidden me to sing back in 1973. And we shared the same spirit, with the same impulse for liberation. Maybe this human impulse for self-determination and dignity was the constant I was looking for? Sometimes we are blind to it, other times we open our eyes and realize that, as my father had said, anything is possible, that we don't have to leave the world as we found it.

The next morning, the UC Berkeley police brought in police from Alameda County to help remove the protesters. We knew it was going to get ugly when the police started taping over their name badges. I had been warned by my parents not to get arrested because of my green-card status. Depending on the charges, I could face deportation. I stayed on the outside of the barricade and watched my friends get roughed up and loaded into buses. As dawn was slowly breaking, with every scream of pain, every twisted arm and nightstick to the ribs, the atmosphere grew more and more tense. Tires were slashed, protesters tried to storm the buses, rocks and debris were flying. A last-ditch attempt to peacefully sit down under the arches of Sproul Gate and block the police buses filled with prisoners from leaving campus was met with swinging batons and broken heads. There was blood everywhere. Thirty-one protestors were hospitalized, ninety-one jailed.

The repression was so brutal afterward that no one that spring was in the mood to keep protesting. It nevertheless must have made an impression on the regents, as four months later, on Nelson Mandela's birthday, the University of California System divested its 3.1 billion dollars from the apartheid economy of South Africa. By the end of 1986, hundreds of universities had followed suit and congress had overridden Reagan's veto to impose crippling economic sanctions on the apartheid regime. I was delighted to hear later that on a visit to the Bay Area right after his release from prison in 1990, Mandela, addressing a crowd of 58,000 at the Oakland Coliseum, celebrated the essential impact of our protests in bringing down the apartheid regime. We had made history.

It was probably a blessing in disguise that the protests subsided because I had come to Berkeley to study, after all. There were many different classes I wanted to take, and five courses per semester was not enough to even begin to satisfy my burning curiosity. I remember taking *Anthropology of Jokes* with the famous folklorist Alan Dundee, who pushed the boundaries of respectability and probably would not have survived the age of political correctness; *Existentialism in Film and Literature* with Hubert Dreyfus, the author of the controversial early classic on artificial intelligence, "What Computers Still Can't Do," although probably more controversial to us was his refusal to teach Sartre and Camus in a class on existentialism; the *Anthropology of Law*, taught as a senior seminar by Laura Nader, but I convinced her to let me in as a freshman; Greek drama; improvisational acting; film theory classes in French and Italian cinema with weekly 16 and 35mm print screenings of classic gems by Godard, Resnais, Renoir, Antonioni, Fellini and Pasolini straight from the vaults of the Pacific Film Archives; and *Sociology of Social Movements*, a class taught by Todd Gitlin, who had been the president of SDS (Students for a Democratic Society) and a lead organizer of many of the first massive anti-war rallies in the mid-sixties.

Thinking back to that glorious time in Berkeley, painting the word *VENCEREMOS* on that rickety shanty, I'm reminded of how my search for some sense of continuity, even in the midst of dissonance, was such a central theme in my work and in my life. The Sufis, known as mystics in Islam, speak of a long rope we must find and grab onto, generation after generation, holding on tight to those who have come before us and even tighter to those who will come in the future. Even in the chaos of my early twenties and in the madness that was *Bezerkely*, I was still reaching for anything that would guide me out of that twentieth-century labyrinth of lost utopias and crushed generational dreams and into a different kind of century and millennium. I believed that as long as I could hold onto that rope with every inch of my human dignity, the way I held on to the songs of my childhood, everything would be all right. No matter what.

BETRAYED
(Chile, 1989-1990)

"Maybe this isn't home, nor ever was—
maybe home is where I have to go tonight.
Home is the place where when you go there,
you have to finally face the thing in the dark."
Stephen King, *It*

When the cop put a gun to my head, I should have known it was over.

It was past midnight on a hot summer night, and I was wearing nothing but my pajama pants and my reckless anger. Two other cops had my second cousin in a chokehold. His mother was screaming bloody murder, my uncle was having a heart attack and half a dozen neighbors were closing in on the scene. My cousin, who lived next door to my apartment building, had been making out with his girlfriend in the backseat of his car. When the cops drove by, they stopped and proceeded to drag them out, kicking and screaming.

I took a step forward. That was a mistake, the kind of mistake you wouldn't make if you'd grown up in Chile under the dictatorship. The cop was young and scared. He must have seen the anger in my eyes staring back at him, and my clenched fists probably didn't help either. His hand was shaking, his finger was on the trigger.

"Do you want this?" he shouted at me. "Do you want it?"

The barrel of the gun was inches away from my face. I put my hands up and, like a drunk under a cold shower, lowered my gaze to the ground

"No," I said and took a step back.

I should have taken another step and then another and a thousand more until I had crossed the border over to Argentina and gotten the hell out of Chile. But I didn't. There was too much at stake. There was no turning back now.

I had just returned to Chile a few months earlier, in December 1989, to vote in our first democratic presidential election since Allende's victory in 1970. It was the historic moment I'd been anticipating all my conscious life. How long had I been waiting, biding my time in the dark to finally hear the songs of my childhood emerge in the light of day in the land where they were born?

Continuing my 1985 streak of moving every eighteen months or so, in 1987 I transferred from Berkeley (or rather escaped) to Duke University in Durham, North Carolina, to be closer to my family. While I studied theater, in 1988, Chileans voted in a plebiscite, 56% to 44%, to reject Pinochet's bid to be "president' for another eight years, setting up the presidential elections I had come to participate in. On December 14, 1989, Patricio Alwyn, the agreed-upon, middle-of-the-road candidate of a negotiated coalition between seventeen political parties from the left and the center, was elected president with 55% of the votes. I had just graduated from Duke University with a degree in Dramatic Arts and moved to Chile, not just to live, but to create and contribute to what I believed was a much-needed public conversation about how best to incorporate the returning Chilean diaspora into the newly woven fabric of an emerging democratic Chile.

I came with a project inspired by my three years of experience working during the summers at various theaters, such as the Mark Taper Forum in Los Angeles, the Hip Pocket Theater in Fort Worth, Texas, and the San Diego Rep as an assistant director to Jorge Huerta, the godfather of Chicano theatre. I was going to produce, design and direct the play *Mud* by the Cuban-American playwright María Irene Fornés, who had given me the limited rights to translate it and stage it in Chile for its unofficial Spanish-language and Latin American premiere.

In the play, Mae and Lloyd are two young siblings stuck together in the muck of rural poverty. Mae's life is transformed when Henry, a seasonal worker, comes to live with them and begins to teach her how to read and write. Soon, Mae's universe expands, and her wings begin to grow as she learns to write the word "butterfly," while her brother, consumed by his own fears, would rather destroy her than let her be free. In a fit of rage and helplessness, he shoots and kills her when she tries to run away.

If I had more sense, I would have put on a comedy and taken myself less seriously. It might have saved me a lot of heartache in the end. Such an endeavor was bound to create trouble for me, but it made perfect sense at the time. Maybe that's why I had gone to Chile, to feel the heartache and make others feel it too. The play was poetic and tragic, perfect for the times, I thought, and I wanted to connect those two worlds of mine, the USA and Chile, and lay them bare under one roof. I wanted to show Chileans that their pain was not the only pain in the world, that El Norte was not Reagan's shining city on the hill they saw in commercials, that it also had its share of people struggling to transcend poverty and ignorance. Mae also represented the dreams and aspirations of the Chilean youth. It seemed obvious that the return to democracy would be an historical opportunity for those who had been marginalized by the dictatorship and Chile's conservative social mores to finally be given a voice and a seat at the table. Wasn't that why we had fought so hard for seventeen years? To give everyone a voice? To give everyone wings?

Figuratively staring at the barrel of a gun, in those precious early months of my return to Chile, I chose to ignore every ominous alarm bell ringing in my ears. I remember standing in line at the Ministry of Foreign Affairs, waiting to acquire an official document that would waive the import taxes and fees on the belongings I had brought back to Chile. The line was getting longer, tempers were flaring. The crowd consisted mostly of middle-aged Chileans, my father's age, and they were getting impatient and complaining about everything.

I remember raising my voice and saying, "Patience, *compañeros*, we are all in this together."

If there ever was a word that defined the Chilean Revolution, it was *compañero,* which is an affectionate way of bringing together the more formal and political "camarada" (comrade) and the idea of someone you break bread with.

A man turned to me, and shouted, "What *compañeros*? There are no fucking *compañeros* here!"

I should have punched him, but that would have been like punching the Zeitgeist or pissing in the wind. The legacy of the dictatorship should have been clear as day: in Chile, solidarity was dead, and from now on, it was every man for himself, everyone struggling for a piece of the empanada.

I let it go. I had better things to do.

As I started producing the play (translating it with the help of my grandmother Fanny during one of my trips to Buenos Aires), I hoped I was going to get some sort of help in Chile to integrate my dreams into this new national stream. After all, many of those who had lived a similar exile to ours were now in positions of real power and had the opportunity (and the responsibility) to be generous and helpful to those of us young *retornados* who had come from all over the world with foreign degrees, languages, skills and experiences that we thought would further the democratization of our country. So, I went and asked for a little support from the Ministry of Education, including a tax exemption, a place to rehearse, help with printing and publicity—nothing out of the ordinary, I thought. I never knew what bitterness truly tasted like until that day I asked for help. I received nothing from those old family friends. There was no national policy for me and for many of my returned friends who were struggling to make ends meet, teaching English in low-paying jobs, living in cramped, cement-block housing on the outskirts of Santiago, wasting away while the older generation was accumulating political power and nice beach houses with tennis courts and swimming pools. I realized that there was no real official policy to deal with my exiled generation, nor for the young who had grown up in Chile during the dictatorship.

So, I hustled. I convinced the young owners of a punk/rock concert venue called Casa Constitución in the bohemian district of Bellavista to rent me their space in exchange for splitting the box office returns. I also got the Chilean American Institute to print the posters and the tickets. I put on the play with the help of three local actors, and after I received some surprisingly rave reviews from *El Mercurio*, the leading pro-Pinochet, right-wing paper, I went back to the Department of Education to see if it would subsidize a tour of the play across Chile. Again, I was completely ignored. I felt betrayed and pushed aside by people I had known since childhood, by a community of people who had the power to make our return to Chile just a bit easier, just a bit softer so that we wouldn't feel too much like strangers in our own land. A small gesture would have made all the difference.

I was told by my friends that I didn't get any help because I didn't belong to a political party. "That's how the money gets distributed around here," they said.

Maybe I should have joined the Socialist Party, become a rank-and-file member; with patience and reverence I could learn how to slowly compromise my ideals in the name of Chile's economic miracle and watch my country turn into "McChile," as my friend and writer Marc Cooper so brutally wrote in an article for *The Nation* magazine. The truth was that if you listened closely beyond the celebratory noise, the sighs of relief, the quiet rumblings of the military, we were not experiencing a "return to democracy" but a "transition towards democracy." This was a process that left the corrupt 1980 constitution intact, made Pinochet a "senator for life," did not diminish the power of the military and, worst of all, was hailed as a coronation of the neoliberal economic model created by the dictatorship. Chile was on its way to becoming the poster child of global capitalism, enacting policies that not even Ronald Reagan dared to implement at the time, such as privatizing social security and even the water pouring down from the Andes.

Fuck it, I said to myself, and I ran out of my castle, naked and without any armor. I plunged right into this new Chile with the rage and self-destruction of a betrayed lover. All this would sound paranoid and delusional if it weren't for the existence of thousands upon thousands of young Chileans like me who shared my disappointment and alienation in this new "democratic" system. I found them, or they found me. I don't really know. Through an old friend of mine, Tino, who claimed he used to rob banks in Costa Rica to help finance the Sandinista insurrection against Somoza, I was thrown deeper into the middle of the Chilean counterculture. Gay performance artists and painters, rockers and punks, theatre and craft artists, filmmakers and drug dealers, ravers and lunatics, drunkards and poets, they were a loose community that had thrived under the dictatorship and were coming of age in this new transitional moment. While Pinochet repressed all overt political speech, he allowed for the existence of what he believed to be an apolitical and nihilistic underground culture. It was apolitical in the sense that we weren't interested in institutional power (remember, in a dictatorship, to be successful is to be a collaborator), but political in the sense that we saw our lifestyle as a form of cultural resistance to the dictatorship and to bourgeois society as a whole. Sex, drugs, rock 'n' roll . . . and creativity.

Pinochet was smart enough to know that we would never hold any real power. He bet that our self-destructive tendencies would only weaken and dilute our rebellious convictions. We were the hippie sixties, punk seventies, new wave eighties and hip-hop nineties all rolled into one drunken anarchistic "party." In the same way that I had lived on the edge of all those foreign cultures during my exile, my Chilean friends had exiled themselves within their own country, refusing to belong to any political group or socially determined class. They forged their own identities not just from their defiance against the military but also from the marginalization of a hypocritical society. And I plunged in with abandon to join them.

It became obvious to me and to my friends that we were going to have to continue to endure the latent powers of dictatorship for a very long time if we weren't ready to join the mainstream and bend over to receive the glorious gift of free-market democracy. So, what was to become of our rebellious identity? What do you do with yourself if you've only known the margins? Do you join the center? And if you do, who are you then?

No one in this new government of baby boomers was ready to face this existential question. The right had destroyed the country with its fascist paternalism, and seventeen years later, free market in hand, the boomers wanted us, the young, the real victims of their mistakes, to trust them? Old, balding and boring white men in suits and ties? Renovated socialists who frowned at men wearing earrings? New Christian Democrats who voted to keep abortion illegal but had enough money to pay for their lover's abortions? Gentler, right-wing fascists who catered to the poor disenfranchised masses? The Berlin Wall had just fallen, and the world would soon be flattened by the triumph of capitalism. Every old-growth forest cut down to supply Japanese fax machines, every handshake with a murderer, every child abused by the Catholic Church, every new mall filled with useless imported riches, every new compromise by the political elite, every betrayal of their past ideals . . . I welcomed it all as the fulfillment of my apocalyptic vision of a Chile damned to hell.

I had developed a frivolous and cynical view of the world. And just as I once had turned a blind eye, lost in my desire to belong, I had to open that eye and realize that the country I had dreamed of had turned into a nightmare for me and for so many of my generation.

One night, I was caught in a *redada*, a general sweep of dissidents, by a dozen police officers armed with machine guns in the Parque Forestal, a stone's throw away from the spot where my father and mother had almost gotten killed by the police in 1965 while protesting the US invasion of the Dominican Republic. I was hanging out with two of my best friends: Tino, the ex-bank-robber from the Sandinista days now turned TV commercial producer, and Francisco, my roommate, one of the *enfant terribles* of the Chilean artistic underground. He loved to dress like the fictitious Victorian-age Comte de Lautréamont, the alter ego of the damned poet and writer Isidore Ducasse. We were working on an art performance based on the *Les Chants de Maldoror* for the grand opening of the Mapocho Station Cultural Center. Francisco was always in character, wearing his leather boots, his heavy jewels, his long coat and highwayman shirt. The cops didn't care much for it. They threw us on the floor of a bus, stepped on our backs and hit us with the butts of their machine guns all the way to the First Precinct Police Station, one of the most infamous in Santiago because it had been a detention and torture center during the dictatorship. Every unlucky street kid, drug addict and drunk, every trans person, prostitute and petty thief wound up there.

Two hundred of us were sat down in long rows on the floor of an old decrepit gym waiting to be processed by an officer hitting a typewriter with his index fingers so slowly, with such dedication, that you'd think he was getting paid by the word. Every time one of the prisoners with an ambiguous gender identity raised his or her or their hand to go the bathroom, all eyes would turn in their direction, waiting to see which bathroom they slowly strutted into. It didn't really matter; the whistles and catcalls were the same whether they went into the men's or the women's bathroom. When it was finally my turn to face the typewriter, I made one last-ditch attempt to express my innocence, but to no avail. I was booked for disorderly conduct and sent to the general holding pen along with my friends. I remember there was a young street kid there who must not have been more than ten or twelve. The police beat him so badly with a long metal bar that he lay unconscious on the floor all night long.

The atmosphere was tense, and I knew my friends and I stuck out like three sore thumbs. The officers had been giving us weird looks all through the night, and I had a bad feeling about it. It was now early Saturday morning. Usually when you're booked on a Friday night, they send you to the penitentiary along with all the hardened criminals, murderers and rapists. I had only one thought going through my mind as I sat in the middle of that small circle of hell: "How am I going to get out of here?"

Facing the holding pen, beyond the dirty metal bars, there was a larger-than-life, wooden, tribunal-like structure where a lieutenant sat on an oversized, antique, mission-style chair. The whole thing looked like a set for some grotesque surreal opera. And like me, the lieutenant seemed totally out of place. I could tell that he hated everything around him and everything about his duty. He was the classic Chilean officer, plucked at young age from the ranks of the fading aristocracy, tall, blonde with blue eyes. Germans and Prussians had emigrated to Chile in large numbers since the 1880s, influencing everything from the local cuisine to the pointed helmets to the Nazi goosestep parades of the Chilean military and their newly acquired torture techniques. Everyone else around him, police and prisoners alike, were shorter and darker than he was. He would look around with a slight contemptuous twitch to his lips, reminding me of the Turkish general, played by José Ferrer in the film *Lawrence of Arabia*. "Who knows what he must have done to be sent to this dump," I thought. His fingers were particularly telling; he would obsessively rub them against each other, as if trying to cleanse himself of all the filth around him. Meanwhile, my two friends had made a pact. In the event that we were going to be sent to the penitentiary, we would resist any attempt to being moved there. It was better to go to an infirmary, they said, than being taken straight to hell.

I shook my head. We were going to get killed.

Right around dawn, the officers finally called our names. One of them opened the cell door while another announced with relish, "You're going down, sons of bitches. Take off your jewelry."

Shit. We were going to the penitentiary.

Tino immediately went into a karate pose. Francisco followed suit, pretending to get into one. The cops on cue brandished their billy clubs.

"Wait, wait, wait, wait!" I stepped forward and I put my body between my friends and the incoming beating. "Please. Wait. If there is a fine, I'll pay it."

The cops froze in confusion. I carefully slipped through them and stood right under the gaze of the lieutenant. I looked up like a penitent addressing God and spoke to him in a hushed, confessional voice so that no one else could hear me. If there was anything that could now save me, it would be an appeal to Chile's racial divide.

"I don't want to be here. You don't want to be here," I said in a quiet, matter-of-fact. "I have green eyes, you have blue eyes," I continued. "How much?"

He looked at me for what seemed like an eternity.

"I'm sorry," I said. "We made a mistake. Can we please pay the fine and go home?"

I had taken a chance on two of the greatest stereotypes of Chilean prejudice. And that day, like most days in Chile, race and class privilege won the day. I paid the fine with every peso I had in my pocket, and we were set free. My privilege had saved my life. As I walked into the soft morning light, I felt sick to my heart. In order to survive I had reinforced and perpetuated Chile's systemic racism. It was killing every inch of my spirit. At the time, my mind had not been trained to recognize this inescapable dilemma, that no matter where I was in the world—even though I was not "white"— I could not separate myself from the benefits of a white supremacist system. This consciousness only came decades later, with the Black Lives Matter movement.

But back then, at the end of 1990, I knew that my Chilean dream was over.

A few months later my parents were back in Chile, and my father was in the throes of writing *Death and the Maiden*, his now famous play dealing with a woman who recognizes her torturer and proceeds to kidnap him and put him on trial in the middle of her living room. The play was a response, some say a critique, of the way Chile, during its transition to democracy, officially dealt with the legacy of the human rights abuses from the dictatorship. At issue was the decision of the Truth and Reconciliation Commission created by the Chilean government to only investigate human rights violations that ended in death. For the play's protagonist and the thousands of other real victims of the dictatorship still alive but broken, there would be no justice. For them, the commission was a slap in their faces and in the face of any real possibility for reconciliation. My father, just as he had given voice to the voices of the disappeared in his literature during exile, had decided to create an imaginary space where this painful, festering wound would be opened up for all to see, to feel and to talk about. Unfortunately, the country was not yet ready to face the collective responsibility of looking at itself in the mirror.

The play my father called "*un dedo en la llaga*," a finger in the wound, was panned by every critic from the left to the right as the worst play ever written and dismissed as an unnecessary provocation. The new government, which was constituted by the very people with whom my father had shared so much blood, sweat and tears during those days of exile, pulled its support and refused to help fund a nation-wide educational tour. The play went on to win an Olivier Award for Best Play in England and a Tony Award for Glenn Close on Broadway. It would be performed in more than one hundred countries in many languages, from Korean and Turkish to Farsi and Tamil.

But all of this was in the future. At that moment, back in Chile in 1990, listening to my experiences with violence and contempt against my generation, my parents had no idea that *Death and the Maiden* would not be well received in Chile or that the year 1990 would prove to be too much for my little brother Joaquín, who was cracking under the pressure of splitting his life in half between his two adoptive countries or that soon enough it would also be all over for them too. All they knew back then was that I was standing in front of them, painfully confessing that I was going back to the United States and that if I stayed in Chile another day, I was going to wind up in jail or possibly killed. It was plain as the light of day. I had taken the blinders off to face the terrible, tragic truth that I had been so consumed with the myth of the eternal return, so obsessed with my desire to find my way home and to belong that it took me all those years to realize what should have been obvious on the morning of September 11, 1973. Chile had been poisoned forever. The songs of my childhood, songs now considered politically naive, profitable only as commercial jingles or expensive collector's items sold in a flea market, were dead echoes of a time when dreams and reality were one and the same. They were now a testament to my struggle and my defeat.

So, finally, I was left standing at the edge of nowhere, without a country, without a home, without a paradise to dream of. There is nothing quite like the pain of ultimate loss. The burning always continues beneath the surface. I remember filming the Occupy Wall Street movement many years later and recognizing this outrage in the eyes and the voices of thousands of young millennials across the United States who woke up one morning to realize that the country they believed in didn't exist anymore and that their American Dream was dead and gone. Welcome to the human race, I told them from behind the lens of my camera.

I hate to say it. I was twenty-three going on sixty. I was angry, so angry. I was ready to tear what was left of my world apart and burn it to the ground.

NINE DESPERATE LIVES INTERLUDE
(San Diego, Los Angeles, Durham, 1991-1999)

In nine years, I must have lived more than nine lives.

In 1991, I landed back in Durham, North Carolina, just in time to renew my green card and buy a used champagne-colored Toyota Corolla SR5 Hatchback with the insurance money I saved up after crashing my Ford Escort on the Hollywood Freeway back in the summer of 1989, driving into a median island and hitting a pole at 55 miles an hour. I crawled out a window, bleeding, as an angel looked down on me, her long, black, curly hair and almond eyes shining against the purple California sunset. She reassured me that everything was going to be all right, and then disappeared at the very moment a paramedic driving home from a Sunday afternoon picnic stopped to give me first aid; an ambulance later took me to South Central General Hospital. I sat in the examining cubicle dressed in my bloody clothes, thinking of Lady Macbeth as I watched gunshot victim after gunshot victim being wheeled in. A doctor finally came in, looked at my nose, in the shape of a crushed eggplant, and said with a God-like smile, "It's your lucky day. I'm only here once a month doing community service. The rest of the time, people in Beverly Hills pay me a small fortune to fix their faces."

Two years later in Durham—my nose was still never quite the same—I packed my few belongings into the Corolla and headed West in search of fame and fortune, like so many millions before me. I drove down Interstate-40 through Texas with a gas mask hanging from my rear-view mirror as the first bombs rained down on Baghdad, announcing the start of the First Gulf War. I went south to Interstate-10 and coasted all the way to San Diego, where my guitar was stolen from the back of the hatchback along with my high school yearbook and the last memories of my French life. They were lost forever and quickly forgotten, after all I was in California once again, still in love with its amnesia-inducing golden sunsets, and no matter what, I had a plan. My mentor Jorge Huerta, the founder of Chicano theatre studies at UCSD, had invited me to work with him producing cross-border plays between San Diego and Tijuana with his Teatro Máscara Mágica company. It was a small gig that paid my one-bedroom rent while I waited to get a California residency. With that I could start graduate school at the University of California, San Diego, in the fall of 1991. Jorge's was the first bilingual theatre program in the nation. What better way to start my self-imposed exile than to become a theatre director and join a nascent artistic movement that was paving the way for a bilingual United States of America. But it was not to be. At the last minute, the program was defunded, and I was forced to leave my theatrical life behind. Stuck in California without a plan, I did what any lost soul would do: I went to Los Angeles in search of the Hollywood dream.

I reunited with Greg, my roommate from the Berkeley days, and we found a house in Echo Park before gentrification whiteout, surrounded by dozens of Mexican roosters and barking dogs in the night, waking up to the sound of gunshots and the blinding searchlight of LAPD helicopters chasing White Fence gang members into my bedroom lit up like a Christmas Tree. I got a side job reading scripts for producer Thom Mount and his production company and I began to drink heavily from the Hollywood Kool-Aid bouncing around with my sci-fi, Dada-induced screenplay titled "Art Operation 666" under my arm. Every young producer told me they loved it but would get fired if they produced it. Lost in my unfolding fantasies, I plunged into the LA rock 'n' roll scene. Mr. Rodrigo was my stage name as the master of ceremonies for a band called El Magnífico, before grunge was cool. I hung out in places like Coconut Teaser and Canters, and after midnight jam sessions at Al's Bar and Smalls. Heroin was everywhere and coffee was cheap. The only way to get laid was to have long hair or a bald head, and I had neither, just my black leather pants made in Argentina and a green mariachi hat I'd bought from a Russian immigrant on the edge of Santa Monica. There was nothing like listening to lounge lizards Marty and Elaine at the Dresden, crooning *Staying Alive* and eating a chili dog at Pinks on Melrose or a Tommy's Burger after midnight on Rampart, where you could cut gang testosterone with a knife. It sure made those shitty burgers taste so much better than if you were sitting pretty in West Hollywood eating sushi, miles from the grit and the grime and the dangerous vibe of a city about to burn itself up in a riot. It was hard to get what you want with tanks and machine gun turrets guarding Pioneer Chicken supermarket down the street on Sunset to stop the momentary redistribution of wealth the talking heads on television called looting and burning. Bob Marley shot the sheriff and NWA fucked the police. Not even the silence of the Joshua Tree desert was enough to purify my confused life, and so I decided to escape one last time, at the midnight hour, leaving Los Angeles behind like a broken wine glass at a party, this time with no one to blame but myself.

Back in Durham, North Carolina, I started the *Andy Tarhole Players,* an experimental theatre group where I met my first wife, and I ate nothing but peas for a week just to get in character for Buckner's Wayzeck. I burned through it too quickly and wound up in Paris working for Buckner's Woyzeck on the movie set of my father's play *Death and the Maiden* at the historic *Studios de Boulogne* with director Roman Polanski, starring Sigourney Weaver and Ben Kingsley. Back in Durham again, I found a job in a second-hand bookstore selling used records and I took the leap of my life by getting married and buying a small house in a fading working-class neighborhood. I thought getting married, getting a mortgage, getting a job, starting a career in writing screenplays and plays with my father and winning awards and making short films that went everywhere and nowhere would be enough to help me forget that I was left without a country, without an identity, without a community and without a way back home. But thinking was getting me nowhere.

There I was, adrift in the months before my first daughter's birth at the end of the twentieth century, still trapped in its endless cycle of war, revolution, exile and defeat. And I was still haunted by the memory of a Chilean family living in exile in Paris in 1974 that kept a photograph of Pinochet glued to a thick piece of wood. Every day of exile they would hammer a nail into it. They let me do it once, and when I first did it, my heart filled with rage and hate; it felt like the best medicine I had ever taken.

In Durham, I had no idea how to escape from that poisoned well I had dug for myself. I had finally sunk to the bottom.

During every major transition and dislocation in my life, my dreams opened up apocalyptic landscapes and other fantastic worlds that sometimes matched the intensity of a Hieronymus Bosch painting. My dreams were brutal, beautiful and exhausting. Sometimes I dreaded going to sleep; it would feel like jumping off a cliff. But three months before Isabella was born, I sat at the bottom of a well, inviting that darkness to overtake me, when a different type of dream came to me. This one was soft and soothing. And it came with a song, a song I had never heard before. The next day, sifting through a pile of used CDs a customer had just brought in to trade at the used bookstore, one of them caught my eye. I slipped it in the CD player, hit play and there was the song from my dream, a song that had come from a country very far away and that, according to the CD liner notes, belonged to a community of mystical healers called the Gnawa, North African Arabic speakers who practiced spirit possession.

"Go," my wife said, "or you'll regret it for the rest of your life."

One song, that's all it took. One song was enough for me to momentarily leave my wife, who was seven months pregnant with Isabella. I quit my job, liquidated my savings, bought myself a ticket and headed straight to Morocco, a country where I knew absolutely no one, on a dream-induced pilgrimage whose final destination was and probably still is a total mystery to me.

Buenos Aires, Argentina, 1914. Days before my great grandmother Raissa will take her son Adolfo back to Odessa, Russia to visit her relatives. Little did my grandfather know that the start of WWI, the Russian Revolution and Civil War will make it impossible for them to return to Buenos-Aires until 1921.

Santiago, Chile, 1973. My parents, Ariel and Angelica, before the military coup.

New York, USA, 1952. My father, age nine, attends the Howdy Doody Show, a children's' television program transmitted from the Rockefeller Center. It was hosted by Buffalo Bob Smith and Howdy Doody, his red-haired, freckled marionette. My father's smile full of American innocence will not last long. One year later, Julius and Ethel Rosenberg, friends of our family, would be executed and my father would live in constant fear for his parent's lives.

New York, NY, 1953. After being hounded by Joseph McCarthy, my grandfather has just been told by his superiors at the United Nations that he must leave the United States My father knows his American paradise is over.

Santiago, Chile, 1973, a few months before the military coup.

Havana, Cuba, April, 1974. Forced to flee Chile after the military coup, we were given temporary refuge by the Cuban government. Here I am proudly posing with the guerilla uniform worn by the Communist Youth Brigades given to me by revolutionary icon, Haydee Santamaria. Photograph taken by my mother on the 20th floor balcony of the Havana Libre, formerly the Hilton. Photo credit: Angélica Dorfman.

Palaiseau, France, 1974. I had started my first year of French school in a small town in the suburbs of Paris, without knowing how to speak or write French. The official school photo could not mask the scar left after I had been beaten up by a band of bullies who apparently didn't like immigrants.

Berkeley, California, 1986. At the Anti-Apartheid protests demanding that the University of California Regents divest their investments from South Africa. I am painting the word VENCEREMOS, the iconic slogan from the Chilean revolution, on a mock shanty town. At the time I was a freshman at UC Berkeley. Photo credit: Pat Miller.

Duke University, Durham, North Carolina, 1988. At the height of postmodernism, protesting President Ronald Reagan's last public appearance with a handmade agit-prop sign, Soviet hat and a Disney Studios t-shirt. I had transferred to Duke the year before where I majored in Dramatic Arts.

Durham, North Carolina, 1988. Chinese Opera make up. Self-portrait with my 35mm Nikon.

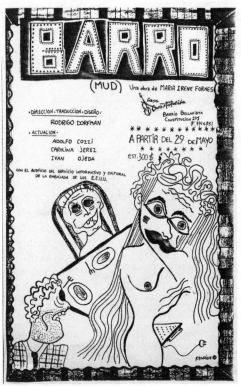

Santiago, Chile, 1991. Poster for the unoficial Latin American premiere of Mud (Barro), by María Irene Fornes.

Berlin, Germany, 1994. Barely hanging on to Marx and the ideological ghosts of the 20th Century. I had tried to dye my hair blonde to play Phoebe Zeitgeist in my theatrical production of Fassbinder's Blood on the Cat's Neck, but instead it turned orange. Marx doesn't seem to care. Photo taken by my father on our way to visit the tomb of Bertolt Brecht in what used to be East Berlin.

Marrakesh, Morocco, 1999. At the famed plaza, Jemma el-Fnaa, playing the role of the dancing fool for the crowd's amusement. Moments before I set the carpets on fire. I had traveled to Morocco in search of the Gnawa, a subculture of mystical musician healers who practiced spirit possession. Photo taken by Pamela Nash.

Carrboro, North Carolina, USA, 2003. Late night Zikr, the Sufi Ceremony of Divine Remembrance. At the time, I was a member of a Turkish Sufi Order.

Turkey, 2007. My last photograph with Sherif.

Durham, North Carolina, USA, 2008. My daughters Catalina and Isabella, right around the time the narrative of this memoir ends.

BOOK III

SONGS FOR A DREAM

Tied in sacks they brought us in camel bags,
And they sold us in the wool market.
May God pardon them.
They took us from our country.
They parted us from our parents.
They brought us, alas, to the wool souk.
And they sold us, children far from our country.

Gnawa song
Transcribed by Christopher Wanklyn

NAILS
(Morocco, 1999)

Looking out north from the ramparts of the Royal Palace, perched high in the Kasbah of Tangier, you can almost reach with your fingertips across the blinding waters of the Mediterranean Sea and touch the shores of southern Spain. I close my eyes and try to imagine Europe as a dream of plenty, full of promise, the way thousands have done before me standing here. After all, it's just a few dozen miles, two lovers almost kissing, close enough to whisper: there is no north or south or east or west here. Just a longing to grasp the invisible and go beyond a pretty postcard.

I remember that morning cab ride from the airport. The driver was a skinny rugged man by the name of Aziz. He had a hawk-like face, dark bushy eyebrows and the thinnest of lips. With his straw hat, he reminded me of a thousand Chilean faces I had seen in the past. Chile was colonized, in great part, by Andalusians, who themselves had been colonized by the Moors and Berbers. My grandmother's family names are Saa and Fernández, so there's no telling what kind of blood runs through my veins, without even mentioning that on my mother's paternal side there was also Middle Eastern blood from the Balkans and Greece. I commented to Aziz on this historical connection. He smiled and swore to me, with all the seduction of a seasoned storyteller, that on a good day if you stood on the ramparts of the royal palace, you could smell the scent of oranges blossoming in the gardens of Cordoba, Spain. He gave me a serious look in the rear-view mirror and then laughed at the marvel of his words time-traveling through the centuries in a mere second. He pulled a key from under his shirt while we waited at an intersection for a green light and held it up just enough for me to notice that it was long and elegantly engraved with intricate floral patterns in the shape of thorns and roses.

"*La llave de mi casa en Granada,*" he said, turning his head in my direction, his eyes lighting up as he savored the rusted scent of its ancient metal.

I smiled back. I knew what he meant. Five hundred years had gone by and Aziz still possessed the keys to the house his ancestors were forced to leave behind after their expulsion from Andalusia in 1492. I thought of all the places I had lived since 1973 and the keys I had lost along the way. None were so beautiful, none so romantic. I nodded in appreciation. He kissed his treasure and lovingly placed it back against his heart with a pat.

The moment soon vanished in a cloud of dust and a near crash with an overturned donkey cart spilling dozens of cracked watermelons on the road. He cursed in Arabic, I cursed in French. Silence. Morocco already resonated like an old friend.

I took my eyes off the coastal line of Spain and looked around: a child sat silently with her older sister peeling oranges, anxious for a bite. An old man stood a few feet away from me, his worn fingers twined behind his back. The cool autumn wind whirled around him, gently lifting his long gray hair; he seemed to be floating in his dark woolen *djellaba*; around him, the soft rays of the sun caressed his rugged face. He could have been thirty or sixty.

Age in Morocco felt like an everyday uncertainty. The young seemed old and the old seemed ancient and the ancient young again. He turned to me and nodded. I nodded back. What was he thinking of? His son gone north? The carved doors of Cordoba? The beauty of the Way, the *Sirat al Mustaqim*? We both looked out to sea. I tried to hear the immigrant songs his son might be

singing and smell the orange blossoms blooming in the garden of
Aziz the cab driver spoke of, but all I could hear was the echo of
crashing waves below. I took another photograph. The exotic
crept again into my consciousness as my "unofficial" guide Leyla
tugged at my shirt. She wanted to go on.

"*Ga me weg?*" she said in her half-broken Dutch. "*Alles gut,
ya, alles gut?*" All good, yes? All good? It was by far her favorite
expression.

I turned to Leyla. She was dressed in a blood red kaftan. She
had a giant mole on her nose and was missing a few teeth. She
had just taken me for a rollicking ride across the *souks* and mar-
kets of the medina and the twisted alleyways of the kasbah. It
was not exactly what I had in mind for my first hours in Morocco.
I had promised myself I would try to land softly, give myself time
to taste and chew the colors and smells of Tangier. And there I
was, not having slept for two days, trying to rest for a few precious minutes, but spurred on by an increasingly paranoid guide
whose idea of a having a quiet cup of coffee was to take me to an
old hippie haunt called Ali Baba's, where hallowed ghosts smack-
ing their lips and tapping their veins offered me heroin and the
possibility of young boys for the night. I remember mumbling
something about my veins being too slippery as we quickly made
our exit.

I could tell stopping, even for a minute, made Leyla uncomfortable. She looked back at me with a frown that seemed to twist
her whole face into a wet rag, the pain pouring through her pitch-
dark eyes, that inscrutable pain of hunger that comes from being
a survivor. She claimed to know the price of every decision she
had ever made: the daughter she had to leave behind, the dangerous voyage north, the cold winters in Holland, the husband
who gave her residency and daily beatings, the money she saved,
the money she lost, the return, the challenge of being a hustler
and a single woman in Morocco. And now that I had forced her
to stop running, stop moving, she had all of a sudden become
very tired and worn.

"*Een minute, asjeblieft . . .*" I tell her in Dutch. One more minute. I didn't want to leave yet. I wanted to squeeze every last drop of the Straits of Gibraltar into my consciousness. I wanted to remember that moment. She threw her hands up in the air and sat down on a rock with a half operatic groan.

I had no idea where I was or how to get back to my hotel. To make things worse, some tough-looking guys were now checking out my backpack and my camera with none too friendly eyes. Leyla's paranoia was becoming infectious, twisting the world into a blur. The events of the day were slowly disintegrating, and I needed to get a grip. Quickly. What the hell was I doing here? What was I looking for?

I had met Leyla a couple of hours after my arrival in Tangier. No map, no *Lonely Planet Tourist Guide* for me, all I needed was a general orientation, I thought, and let life do the rest. I'll take my chances. Anyway, the guidebook had already been wrong about one thing: the train station was no longer in the Ville Nouvelle, but had been moved to the outskirts of town to make way for a hotel and casino complex. Before going to my hotel, Aziz, the cab driver, had taken me from the airport to the new station, which was nothing more than a miniature cement block in the middle of a sea of gigantic half constructed high rises in a low-rent neighborhood, where mounds of trash piled up in corners and literally hundreds of school children and as many chickens were crossing the street with impunity. I bought my ticket for that night's train to Marrakesh, my final destination.

I asked the attendant why the station had been moved. He laughed and shook his head with a wry smile, sharing with me the absurdity of his situation. "I have to take an extra bus to get here," he said in French. He shrugged his shoulders. "Politicians. . . ."

Twenty minutes later, I checked in at the hotel El Muniria, famed for being the place where William S. Burroughs wrote *Naked Lunch*, the infamous book that had once been banned, just like my father's *Donald Duck* book. Both had been deemed too dangerous for bourgeois sensibilities. It occurred to me that I could try and catch Burroughs's ghost. At the hotel desk, I was received by the owner, Peter, a quirky Englishman, and proceeded to follow him up a steep stairwell to the second floor, where I was ushered into a non-descript room where Jack Kerouac used to stay when he visited Burroughs. The myth or lie immediately pulled me in.

A giant palm tree stirred against one of the open windows. Behind it you could see the minaret of the local mosque and, further on, the harbor of Tangier with its deep blue sea scintillating like a daytime cosmos. The other window overlooked the narrow Rue Magellan and the competing hotel across the street with a maze of stairs and alcoves leading to a cozy rooftop café, where a couple of young, hip-looking Moroccans were listening to blaring pop music and rolling what looked like a big fat joint.

"I'll take it," I said to the owner. "If it's not ready, I can wait. All I really need is a shower."

An older Moroccan woman peeked inside the doorframe and frowned. Fatima was the deaf-mute maid of the hotel. She was really the one in charge, it seemed. She and Peter got into an argument filled with grunts and gestures mixed with Peter's exasperated invocations of "for God's sake."

After a quick shower, I left the room to roam around Tangier and get a bit of fresh air in the hopes that it would put me to sleep later that afternoon. But Burroughs' ghost wouldn't let me get off that easy. The key to the room was twice as long as the door was thick and more difficult to manipulate than the English language. I imagined Kerouac coming back to his room in the thick of a dark night, high as a kite, trying to open that damn door. There he was: —key—door—the East—must open and take a piss. There I was, forty years later. People come and go but doors never change.

I walked up a steep hill, up a narrow stairwell-street covered in trash and bird shit, splattered like a Jackson Pollock where a small group of African immigrants huddled together waiting to be smuggled to Spain on a small fishing boat in the dead of night.

With the occasional whiff of urine in the air, I slowly ascended towards Avenue Mohammed IV, one of the main arteries of the Ville Nouvelle, the newly built part of the city. There would be no map for me that day. I just knew that I needed to make a right turn, and then a series of meanderings and labyrinths would lead me to the Great Door of the Old Medina and what was advertised as a lively and colorful plaza called Le Petit Souk, the little market. My earlier attempts back at the hotel to follow the written directions in the guidebook had proven to be not just dizzying but also completely incomprehensible. They felt like some secret language not meant for the impurity of my Western eyes. So, I assumed the role of dyslexic rat in the Moroccan maze.

To my surprise, as I took those first steps, I suddenly experienced a wave of recognition and complicity that left me almost paralyzed in my contemplation of the strange and yet familiar surroundings. Tangier smelled and resonated like the port city of Valparaiso in Chile, a place I had visited and explored many times in the previous sixteen years; it was a place I knew I would take my daughter Isabella to visit one day and that she would fall in love with it, just like I had. It was as if all ancient Third World port cities built on hillsides shared that same primal energy; they were all burned, colored and salted into the landscape.

Tangier is like a series of planes that intersect and dissolve, where the unbearable freshness of the sea air mixes with the sweet fragrance of rotting fish and 19th-century French urban architecture, fried liver, cold native stares, diesel fumes, all to the tune of Moroccan Arabic dialects, Berber, Spanish and French, heaps of tender mint leaves and warm fennel cakes, giant bugs emerging from cracks in the sidewalks, hot in the sun, cool in the shades. It was as if I had been there before, the senses obliterating the very definition of a contradiction, every step leaving nothing behind but the faint recognition of the few preceding seconds, minutes — or was it centuries?

All I knew was that my pilgrimage was not just one last wild escapade before becoming a father, one last chance to reaffirm my belief that dreams can come true. No, there was something else I was looking for, but I didn't know what it was. Not yet, at least. All I knew was that I wanted to meet up with the Gnawa, the mystical brotherhood of healers and musicians who had hundreds of chapters across Morocco. I had gathered the little information I knew about them from a few disparate CD liner notes. One of them on the Axiom label, was called *Gnawa Music of Marrakesh Night Spirit Masters.* From what I had read, the Gnawa traced their lineage to the thousands of black African slaves who were brought to Morocco starting in the 1500s with the fall of Timbuktu. Their music was often marketed and catalogued by Westerners as "trance music," and their syncopated rhythms, created by large metal castanets called *krakebs*, could reach, just like techno, up to a staggering 120 beats per minute. It is still performed in all-night rituals of spirit possession called *lilas,* in which the community comes together, sacrifices a goat or a cow, cooks and eats it and then performs music and dances all night long to call forth various spirits from the Arab and African pantheon. Each spirit has its own color and story as well as its own healing power.

I had brought along a tape recorder with the intention of creating a sound journal of my voyage to share with my daughter one day. In a way I didn't want to fall prey to the experiential trap of substituting a photograph for the real thing. Documenting marginal groups has been a traditional genre since the early days of "salvage ethnography," when Western anthropologists roamed the colonized world anxiously trying to capture on film the rapidly vanishing cultures being displaced by white people's "superior" civilization. With tape recorder in hand, I had come to listen more than anything.

I had finally made it to the Petit Souk and stopped to get a drink from a small tea house overlooking the marketplace. The few tables in the shade were taken and, inside, every single chair was occupied by men sipping tea, watching a soccer game on television. As I stuck my head in, they all turned at once to look at me. I quickly walked around the front, got myself a Fanta and went to take a seat outside in the blistering sun, when I saw a woman sitting in the shade motion to me with her index finger to join her. At first, I pretended not to notice her, but she insisted by waving her whole hand and then calling to me with a deep voice. I had been warned against fake guides and yet I couldn't blame her; I was the only tourist in the vicinity. I walked up and sat down next to her in the shade. Her name was Leyla. All I could think of was "Layla," that catchy Eric Clapton tune.

She didn't speak French but understood some Dutch. Since I had lived four years in Amsterdam in the mid-seventies, I could wrangle enough words and expressions together to create the semblance of a conversation. I bought her a soda and offered her a cigarette. She gave me a disapproving stinky-cheese face, as if she didn't have time or money to smoke it. She asked me if I wanted to visit the souk and the kasbah. Guides made extra money by taking a tourist straight to a predetermined store, where the unsuspecting victim would get fleeced with overpriced souvenirs. The point was to catch a tourist on their first day before they could compare prices and get a grip on the market. I told her that I was tired and wasn't in the "tourist" mode of buying anything. I was looking for the Gnawa. She said she knew where to find them, and I was foolish enough to believe her.

We spent the next couple of hours zigzagging upwards to the top of the kasbah, visiting stores and saying, "No thank you," to every possible rug, trinket and souvenir. By the time Leyla announced she would take me to see a Gnawa, I was tired and didn't think it was a good idea. She plowed ahead anyway and led me to a dusty corner, up some broken steps and into an ancient-looking loading dock. She knocked on an old decrepit door with a roughly painted sign that read "GNAOUA," the French spelling of "Gnawa."

The door opened ajar and the head of a man emerged from the darkness. His face was all puffed up as if he had just gone to sleep after a night of heavy drinking, and his hair looked like a tumbleweed. He squinted and recognized Leyla. From the tone of his voice, I gathered he told her to go to hell and never come back. Without skipping a beat, Leyla ignored him, took me by the hand and dragged me up the kasbah to the edge of the ramparts of the royal palace, where some young Moroccans who had been eyeing my backpack were now making hissing sounds, warning me that if I didn't leave soon, something bad was going to happen.

A wave of exhaustion and thirst came over me, and I signaled to Leyla that I was ready to go back to the hotel. One of the Moroccans took out a knife. Leyla grabbed my arm and dragged me away without a word. I looked back one last time. The sun was slowly setting, Spain was disappearing in a mist, two dark hostile figures were eyeing me and the only Gnawa I had seen told me to go to hell.

This sense of defeat became painfully clear as we made our way back down to the Petit Soul looking for a place to exchange my dollars for some Moroccan cash for Leyla. Her paranoia and her fear of the police were peaking, and she forced me to walk ten feet behind her and pretend we did not know each other. She had warned me that guides like her without official licenses were severely punished by a special police unit called the Brigade Touristique. When we finally got to the hotel, I gave her one hundred dirhams ($10), which was the amount the tour book suggested I pay a fake guide. Of course, Leyla argued for more. I refused. She suddenly became very agitated, her expression quickly turned to rage. She yelled that she was hungry and that her children back home had nothing to eat. A few passers-by stopped and watched her public display with disapproval. An older Moroccan gentleman wearing a worn-out striped suit and carrying a long rolled up carpet assured me, in French, that I had given her plenty and that he knew her.

"She is a whore," he said with a grimace: "*Une putain.*" He chased her away with a flick of the wrist, like one does with a swarm of flies.

I watch Leyla turn around and leave, cursing everyone around her, including me. What was I to believe? Did Leyla invent all her stories? Was this the price she had to pay for being a single woman in Morocco? In a flash, the extent of her misery had been revealed, and I was now a part of her narrative, I was the ugly tourist who had cheated her. I was the ghost of her colonial past.

I sat there on the steps of the hotel for what seemed like hours, trying to calm my racing heart, but to no avail. The damage had been done. Leyla had captured me in her gaze, defined me on her terms, and I wished I had given her those extra ten dollars she had said she needed.

"Where are you from?" a familiar voice interrupted my guilt-infused reverie.

I looked up. It was Peter, the owner of the hotel. "Chile," I said.

"Really . . ." he muttered to himself. "Two girls from Chile spent the night here last night. They're going to Marrakesh tonight."

One of the golden rules of exile was that in general there were two kinds of Chileans traveling outside the country: collaborators and exiled friends. Whenever you heard that typical Chilean accent vocalized in public by someone you didn't know, you were supposed to become immediately anonymous and silent until they left your vicinity. This fear was due in part to the fact that Pinochet had sent agents to Europe to track down and infiltrate the Chilean resistance and even possibly kill activists like my father. They certainly had succeeded with the car bombing and murder of our family friend Orlando Letelier and his assistant Ronnie Moffit on Embassy Row in Washington, DC in 1976. As a matter of survival, distrust was considered a virtue, separation a necessity. Here I was in exile, unable to return to our country, unable to visit our relatives and friends, cut off from the smells and colors that gave me birth, and was I about to encounter wealthy right-wing tourists or government officials who had looted our country and were subsequently free to come and go as they pleased? How could I not anticipate feeling disgust and hate?

"They went to have a drink next door," Peter added. "They want to meet you. You're also going to Marrakesh tonight, aren't you?"

I went up to the same funky terrace overlooking the port I had seen from my hotel window what seemed like ages ago. It was buzzing with young, hip Moroccan swingers in fashionable leather jackets, enamored couples barely touching hands under the stern gaze of an elderly chaperone, families with children and teeny boppers out from school. Arab pop music blared from hidden speakers. Everyone was drinking mint tea. The call to prayer from the minaret of a nearby mosque could barely be heard over the pop music.

I picked them out of the crowd: two platinum blondes, sticking out like a wildfire, but they were definitively not from Chile. Pamela and Greta were two cousins from Northern California, and they looked remarkably fresh and mellow for being on the last leg of a two-month trip around the Mediterranean. We hit it off, and they invited me for appetizers and drinks at London's Pub, one of the last relics of Burrough's *Interzone* with a portrait of Queen Victoria, circa 1956, hanging on the wall. Pam and Greta had been there the night before, and Youssouf, the owner, had taken a liking to them and invited them to come again. Bottles of wine came and went, and all sorts of tiny and exotic tapas were offered and eaten. A few hours passed. Youssouf mentioned that the bartender, a tall gaunt man, was an actor who had starred as one of the mummies in a recent Hollywood film.

"He was one of the guys in gauze," Youssouf blurted out excitedly and asked the bartender to go home and get his album of photographs.

We said that it wasn't necessary and that it was almost time to go the train station, but Youssouf insisted. It took the barman more than half an hour to get his album. And yes, there he was photo after photo with Hollywood stars, wrapped like an ancient mummy.

We barely made it to the train station and boarded the famous "Marrakesh Express"—old, smelling of rusted metal and as loud as any train I'd ever taken. First, its blaring horn moaned like a camel in heat, and then its brakes screeched for five, long interminable minutes, like an extended aria of some perverse desert opera. There was nothing "express" about that train, which seemed to stop at every small, obscure, apparently inhabited sand-filled station along the way. At each stop I lay on my cot in agony for some sort of movement. Only when the train began to move again was there any chance of drifting back into a slumber relentlessly punctuated by the deafening noise of the locomotive.

Finally in Marrakesh, I found my way to the famous medieval square of Jemaa el-Fnaa, which in Arabic means the gathering of self-oblivion, because it was where criminals were once beheaded. Perfect. I was obviously insane and had already lost my head. The moment I stepped into the plaza, I got sucked into a street performance in which an old man, wrinkled and wiry with a long fairy-tale-like beard, played the same vaguely discordant song over and over again on a Berber one-string fiddle while he told who knows what fantastic tales from his life. He had with him a magical prop: a beaten-up, vintage, hand-cranked, portable Victrola. The old man would ceremoniously stand up, crank the player and play a 78-rpm recording that he claimed to have recorded in the 1940s with a French ethnomusicologist who had wandered into his village. Someone next to me translated tidbits of his story. The moment the performer saw the exotic blondes, Greta and Pam, he invited us to sit down next to him and join the show. I recognized the pattern: invite tourists and make fun of them at their own expense because they don't understand the language or the raunchy jokes. Why not turn power relations upside down and allow these folks a momentary respite from centuries of colonial oppression? And surely Europeans could also use the opportunity to wash away some of that nagging guilt?

The old man would sing a couple of lines in Berber, the native language of the Atlas Mountain region, and I was able to sing them back, imitating him. People were impressed enough to start tossing what seemed like a lot of money in our direction. Coins were raining down on us like dirhams from heaven. After a little while, the crowd had grown considerably larger. I took his hat and started asking for money in his name, all the while pretending I was a donkey who could speak five languages, braying in Italian, Dutch, French, English and Spanish. People seemed amused.

Someone asked me who I was and where I came from. One of my favorite answers in this type of performative situation was to raise my hand to the sky and point my index finger to the heavens as if I were a fallen angel.

"Don't we all come from the heavens?" I declared.

I felt emboldened in my sleepless euphoria and imagined myself the bastard child of a medieval minstrel, a cosmic performance artist. I began to tell stories of my exile in France and how I wound up speaking, like them, French, the grand oppressive language of the colonialists.

"We are strangers, but are the same," I said, my emotions naked to their eyes.

And then, as if there was no other way out, the story of my mother trying to buy ham in Paris came out. I told them how she went to the local butcher and in her Latin American accent asked for "*yanbon*," and how the butcher treated her like a child, just the way the French treated them and their country. The words flowed like a litany of despair, like a prayer for understanding, about all the ways children suffered in the throes of history, how they were the victims of an unjust adult world and how the audience members should love their children. And with that, I bowed and stepped out of the circle. But before I could leave, the old man stood up and spoke. Someone translating the old man's words told me he wanted me to perform with him again. He wanted me to be his partner, go into the mountains with him, and we would split the earnings. Everyone applauded.

What an offer!

When would I ever get another opportunity like that? Imagine, traveling with an old Berber musician, from village to village, deeper and deeper into the Atlas Mountains, getting lost until I was born again. He probably offered the job because at some point I was telling the crowd that I had lost my plane ticket and was washing dishes at the Hotel Ali to pay for my way back home. I was joking, but he must have believed me. I respectfully declined, I told him I had come looking for the Gnawa and, with that, I left the circle with Greta and Pam.

As we crossed the square, we finally found a group of Gnawa musicians and dancers performing for tourists. I watched them in sheer delight and gave them some money. They put a colorful cap on my head and invited me to dance with them. Everybody was entertained until I tried to do a semi-Russian crab dance backwards and hit one of their kerosene lamps with one of my arms, breaking it and starting a small fire.

General pandemonium ensued. The crowd was loving it.

I kept on dancing and afterward gave them enough money to buy a new lamp. No matter how much fun I was having, I was still a tourist. I knew I wanted more. I wanted to go deeper. But how do you go past the postcard, beyond the tourist trap, beyond exoticism, colonialism, orientalism and every other "ism" that had marked my life? Maybe I had it all wrong? Maybe I needed to wait until they found me? So, I did exactly that. I sat at the grand Café Etoile Glacé on the edge of the square and waited.

And it happened.

I made friends with Mohcine, a twenty-something Moroccan who wanted to practice his English. He was educated and curious. He knew about Chile and about the music of the great Chilean singer and martyr Víctor Jara, who was executed in the soccer stadium turned concentration camp in the days following the military coup. According to Mohcine, Víctor Jara had greatly influenced the Moroccan protest singers of the 70s. We joked around and liked each other immediately.

That night when he invited me (and my traveling companions, Pam and Greta) to his home deep in the labyrinth of the kasbah, I found to my delight that his mother, Malika, was a Gnawa priestess who danced with fire and practiced spirit possession. In one short breath, I confessed to her that I had traveled to Marrakesh precisely to witness that type of celebration. To my surprise, she said she had been planning a *lila* for weeks and that, if Pamela, Greta and I contributed $200, she would pitch in another $100 and organize a ritual celebration in two days' time. Mohcine would make sure every dollar was accounted for. We needed a black goat, but without spots, because the black *mlouks*, spirits of the African forests, liked them that way; and a red rooster to please Sidi Hammou, the red spirit of the slaughterhouses. There needed to be seven types of incense, for the seven houses of the spirits. She also needed colored shawls for the color of each spirit and rose water to sprinkle on those coming out of possession.

It would be an intimate gathering: in addition to us, she'd bring her family, the musicians and dancers and a few friends who would help her channel the various spirits called up that night.

"And, if you have any psychological problems, the spirits will cure them," Malika promised without hesitation.

Two days later in a small, two-story cement house on the dusty outskirts of Marrakesh, I was allowed to witness how a community shares its joys and its sorrows in ways I had never experienced before. The doors of mystical Islam opened for me that night, and I went right through them into a succession of dances and colors, incenses and music associated with the various spirits living in the large pantheon of the Gnawa cosmology. I was told how each spirit was invited to descend from the ether by playing its favorite song and burning its particular incense. The spirit would enter the tip of a metal leaf attached to a three-stringed lute played by the Gnawa master musician and into the bodies of those called upon to enter into possession. It was an even exchange: the spirit gains a body for a few minutes, experiencing the pleasures of the senses, and the dancer is cleansed or "filtered" of all negativity by the visiting presence as it makes its way through the dancer's body. The spirit leaves satisfied, the dancer collapses, sometimes howling, sometimes crying in purified ecstasy.

It was intoxicating. From the moment I saw Hassan the dancer earlier that day I was struck by his presence. He was slim and athletic, with long, androgynous, chiseled features and thick eyebrows, always quiet and soft spoken, his eyes revealing only the outer edges of his hidden essence. After the sacrifice and the cooking of the goat meat (the raw heart saved for Sidi Mimoun, the powerful black spirit of the forest) the ritual itself began with loud drumming and acrobatic dancing. Then, the multicolored vagabond spirit known as Dedebella and the white spirit known as Abdel Kader Gilani opened the gates to let in the green spirits belonging to the house of the Prophet Mohamed. As I watched grandmothers wailing into possession, literally pulled into the center of the crowded room by their spirits to dance chaotically like possessed puppets on invisible strings, sometime in the dead of the night, when the blue spirit of Moses and those who swim across the waters arrived, Hassan began to dance. He undulated with a bowl of boiling water and mint leaves placed on top of his head and, as the music and the dance reached a crescendo, the bowl of mint tea suddenly fell and spilled onto the carpet.

Silence. Everyone froze.

Hassan gasped for air as if coming up to the surface after a long, tunneling swim and dropped to the ground, his face twisting in agony. He had broken the connection with his spirit and was feeling the pain of the unwanted separation. Quickly, his friends helped him up, filled the bowl and gently encouraged him to start again. The music picked up intensity, the incense clouded the room and, as if nothing had happened, he lowered himself to the ground and began to undulate again with the bowl still on his head as if a continuous stream of waves were shaping his body into liquid form. After a long swim, he slowly emerged, stood up and finished his dance as calmly as he had begun it. One of the helpers gently took the bowl of infused mint water and offered it around the small room. The earlier mistake had given Hassan's dance a powerful dramatic arc, and we all had wanted him to succeed.

As I took a drink from the bowl he had carried on his head with such care, I felt a growing feeling of tenderness. Someone placed a blue shawl on my head and gently invited me to join the other three participants by dancing in front of the musicians. My head bowed, I began to follow the steps I had seen others take. Slowly at first, two little hops to the right and then two little hops to the left, a gentle swaying, a calming sea. I was at peace. The music began to intensify and so did my dancing. As I was breathing in that blue incense, my mind began to wander away, my body felt tired, exhausted, spent, as if I was ready to let it all go, calmly and peacefully, like a drop falling into the ocean.

To dance with those women, those daughters, mothers, grandmothers, truly made me feel like I was home again. I had returned, but not to the place I had imagined. I suddenly felt taken by a powerful force that brought me to my hands and knees. "Submit," I heard a voice inside of me say. "Let yourself go."

My breathing was long and deep, and I suddenly collapsed on the floor. The sounds of the room seemed faraway like a lullaby of waves crashing in a distant sea. I opened my eyes. Hassan had fallen next to me, his body shaking, his eyes rolling back inside his head, white, unrecognizable. His hand fell on my chest, but I could not move. I remember curling up like a child, my head on Pam's lap, and I began to cry.

I thought of Chile and how I was robbed of the possibility of having a community like the Gnawa, how I would never be part of an ancient tradition . . . any tradition . . . or know the deep meaning of belonging. I cried for my father and my mother, who had lost Chile, and my grandfather who had lost Russia and Argentina, and my daughter Isabella, and the family's curse of exile she was about to be born into and that my brother Joaquín had been unable to escape. All the anger and sadness of the past twenty-five years came out like a river pouring into the sea of that night when I let myself go with those beautiful strangers in their spiritual world. I finally understood why that song had brought me to that little house on the outskirts of Marrakesh: I had come to hear an agonizing truth. Every single hate-filled nail on that picture of Pinochet, back in Paris, every angry slam of that hammer, turned out to be a nail driven straight into myself. And if I didn't find a way to take them out, one by one, those nails would begin to pierce my daughter Isabella the moment she was born. Like the Gnawa, I had to find a way to heal, a way to live, to cry and to laugh with my demons.

I wanted to break the spell.

I wanted a clean slate.

BOOK IV

SONGS FOR A NEW HOME

Gracias a la vida
Thanks to life

Violeta Parra

AMERICAN SUFI
(North Carolina, 1999)

"I've converted to Islam," I told my father.

He nodded and said nothing. We hadn't seen each other in a couple of weeks, and I'm sure this was not what he was expecting when I told him I needed to talk to him.

"I joined a Sufi Order that I found just ten miles from here, in Chapel Hill . . . the week after I came back from Morocco. It's an amazing community made up of Turks and Americans. And there's also a few members from Azerbaijan and Uzbekistan. Our teacher is called Sherif. I like him. A lot. We dance and we pray, and I'm learning how to sing in Turkish. I've never experienced anything like it," I said in one single breath.   I   must   have sounded like I had lost my mind.

We were sitting across from each other at Elmo's, the local family restaurant, ready to order lunch. I could see his mind racing a thousand miles an hour trying to find the right words. After all, as a writer, words are his bread and butter. It was only fair that I should let him sit with mine for as long as it took him to find his. The waitress came, and he ordered his chicken spinach salad with extra walnuts on the side. I ordered a cheeseburger, a Caesar salad and a lemonade.

"So, tell me more," he finally said, carefully bringing the palms of his hands together so he could rest his chin on his thumbs and put his elbows on the Formica table.

131

"I know. Why in the world would a fourth-generation atheist with an impeccable revolutionary pedigree want to become a Muslim?" I said teasingly.

He smiled. "Yes, why?"

"So glad you asked. Let me tell you why. Remember when I told you and Mom that if I stayed in Chile I was going to get myself killed?"

"Yes, I remember that very well."

"Well, it's the same. I need to change the narrative of my life. Right now. Or else I'm not going to make it."

"What do you mean?"

"It's the end of the twentieth century, Dad. I'm done with communism, socialism, capitalism and every other kind of useless *ism* that has shaped my life into a prison of hate and resentment. I'm done. I'm all dried up. Like an old prune, as Rumi would say. I'm jumping off this runaway train before it crashes into a dead end, because that's the only thing it has to offer. A dead end. I've run out of words to express who I am, what I want to do with my life and how I want to raise my children. I've run out of songs and metaphors and images I can dream of. I need to find another way to shape my world or else I'm going to die. Spiritually."

"I understand. So, you believe in God?"

"It's complicated."

"I believe in angels," my father said softly, as if the mere mention made it real.

"Yes, and you're the worst Marxist I know."

"I'm not a Marxist. I'm a democratic socialist who uses Marxism as a tool for critical analysis."

"I know, and you're also a poet. I'm teasing you. Listen, I don't know what 'God' is. I have no idea and I don't care. That's not the point."

"That's not the point?"

"No, the point is: what's the best story for me to live in? Do you know what one of my earliest memories of you is? You would put me to bed, sing me a song you just invented that morning, tell me some fantastical tale and then just as you were tucking me in between the sheets, you would point to the ceiling and remind me that right above me, right there in the night sky, far away, shining bright, was my guiding star. And it was mine, no one else's. Do you remember?"

"Yes. I wanted you to know that you were not alone in the world. That no matter where you were, even after I was dead, you would not be left alone. That you would always have it watching over you, guiding you."

"Well," I continued, trying not to get caught in my father's sentimentality, "do you remember that I used to collect those stickers about the creation of the world? They would come in little packets and then I would stick them in an album?"

"Vaguely."

"The images went from the Big Bang to the formation of the Earth, flowing magma, volcanoes, ice ages, dinosaurs of all shapes and sizes. You bought me a whole bunch when you took me to visit La Moneda two days before the coup. . . . Remember?"

"That I remember. I wanted you to see where Allende worked before . . . before it was all over."

"Yes, anyway, those stickers were like currency at school. We would trade them, gamble them, and I had a good number of them, but there was one, one sticker that no one had. Like nobody. All the stickers were single stickers, but this one, this one was one long sticker. It was the length of five individual stickers and it depicted a Diplodocus standing in front of three red double-decker London buses. And no one had it. I bet you not a single kid in Santiago had it."

"And you had it?"

"No, I didn't have it. I told you, nobody had it. You might as well play the lottery than hope to ever get it."

"And so, what happened?"

"One night, one of those nights when I was left alone in the dark staring at the ceiling, thinking about my guiding star, I decided to talk to it. Like I prayed to it. I had never done anything like that before because I was not sure it was real. You know what I mean? I remember saying something like, please, please, please, give me the long sticker . . . something like that."

I paused for effect and watched my father's expression. He was listening.

"I was staying at my grandparents . . . maybe you and Mom were on your trip to Cuba when you won that book award. And Chebochi (that's what I called my grandfather Adolfo) had gone shopping, sparing me a visit to the stinky cheese store, and he had brought me a bunch of little sticker packets. I remember I was in bed and I sat up and opened the first one, still half asleep. And there it was, right there, unrolled before my eyes—the long, impossible-to-find sticker."

"I don't remember any of this."

"Right, you were in Cuba. Anyway, my head exploded. I remember I ran down the stairs and out the front door still in my pajamas, down the street, and I knocked on the neighbor's door to show my friend the sticker. I couldn't believe it. You know, in some way I'm still there, in that moment, frozen in time, holding the proof in my hands that my guiding star was real. Is real. Of course, I know it's not about asking for things. I don't believe in God, or whatever you want to call it, because it will answer my prayers. I believe in it because it *did* answer my prayer when I needed to move from having hope to having faith. You know the difference between the two, right?"

"Yes, and *how* I do," my father answered. I think he knew where I was going.

"In Arabic you have the word *burhan*, which means the proof, the evidence of the existence of God," I continued with my scrambled logic. "I've always believed in something bigger than myself, my guiding star, the dream of paradise, of Chile, of revolution, something bigger, something that can help me get my head out of my sorry ass, out of my ego, out of my self-pity and all the terrible things I have done to myself in order to survive. Have you noticed how I'm always escaping, running away the moment I hear the slightest crack in the ice?"

"And you're also a fighter. You stand your ground and you don't give up. You're probably the most stubborn person I know . . . after your mother."

"I fight and then I run away. I've been running away all my life."

"Sometimes you have to. I had to escape Chile in 1973. Do you think I wanted to leave? I didn't. I wanted to die there and be another martyr. But I decided to live. For your mother's sake, for your sake. For the sake of all the stories that needed to be told. I had to. Which meant I had to leave. Just like you had to leave in 1990. As you know, Rodrigo, life is full of impossible choices."

"Yes, and I'm tired of making impossible choices. Or putting myself in situations where I have to make impossible choices. Since I was little, in order to survive, I've had to accept that my body was here but my heart was back in Chile. I could not attach myself to this world because it would mean the betrayal of a possible return. All my life I've lived trying to reconnect with something deep inside of me. That was the prime intention, my essential motivation, the architectural landscape of my mind. After the coup, this desire to reconnect was linked to something specific, temporal. Even if they were blurred dreams of innocence, they had a vague feeling of unity and belonging associated with childhood memories. And so, when I went back to Chile, I stubbornly brought with me the forms I had nurtured in exile . . . and of course it didn't work. It couldn't work. Cultural and historical identities are here to give us a sense of security, yes, but if that security comes at the cost of feeling separate, divided from others, then those identities will bring you nothing but pain and misery. I don't want to be Chilean, I don't want to be an American. I don't want to be anything. I'm grateful that Chile refused me the way it did, that it spat me out like the whale spat Jonah out, and broke my heart. Yes, grateful, because now I can see a deeper truth. It's taken me all these years to see that my attachment to an imaginary Chile was a mistake. It's fruitless to attach yourself to anything temporal in that way. In the end it will betray you; it will stab you in the back. And if you're lucky, you will open your eyes and realize that the heartbreak was actually a liberation from the preconceived, stagnant forms that disfigured your life and held you hostage. After 1990, I thought I had been left with nothing. I was wrong. I was left with something priceless and rare. I was left with the pure essence of longing, the kind of longing that Rumi writes about. Not for a country, or a national identity or even a social utopia no, but for something else."

"And what is that something else?"

"I don't know. It feels like I've found a home *in* the world, and yet I've always known on some level that I've lived my life knowing I was not *of* this world. Does that make sense?"

"Well, your mother has always claimed that she's an extraterrestrial from another planet . . . so, who am I to argue?"

"Right. I've lived my whole conscious life in political exile, and now I'm ready to make the jump and embrace the bitter sweetness of what I call my cosmic exile. I want to be like Rumi, comfortable in hell while dancing on the edge of the roof. I want to feel the flood inside of me and be the ark that tames and guides my inner animals one by one to safety. I want to feel the reality of a metaphor. I want to bring all the contradictions of my life under one roof and be content with the fate I have chosen. I have to come to terms with what I've been given and accept it for what it is. I have to submit. That's what Islam means, ultimately: to submit."

My father looked at me for a long time and said something I will never forget, because in that moment he was sending a message to my future self, when I would have to make one of those impossible choices that keeps breaking me into little pieces.

"Rodrigo, I just need to know one thing . . . so that when I tell your mother all of this we can rest assured. This teacher, this Sherif of yours, do you feel like you can tell him the truth? No matter what?"

I answered without thinking. "Yes, of course."

"Then everything will be all right."

Ten years later, his words came back to haunt me in ways that I could have never imagined.

BEST OF INTENTIONS
(North Carolina, 1999-2008)

The wound is the place
where the light enters you.
Rumi

Isabella Angelica Chiti was born on the first day of my first Ramadan. Her eyes wide open, she was ready to shatter my world with her existence.

The thirst, the hunger, the self-awareness, the empathy, the lack of sleep and the meditative qualities of fasting made the surface of everything around me shine and shimmer during those early days as if I lived awake in dreams. I was ready to be shattered because it was *my* shattering, my script, my movie, my self-discipline. My choice. My story.

I had returned from Morocco with a spark. And now back in North Carolina, I was a raging forest fire burning with the intensity of a convert on the road to Damascus. Sherif became my sheikh, my master, my spiritual teacher, my link to a chain of direct transmission from master to student since the dawn of Islam. Reborn, like everyone else, I was given a Sufi name. Mine was (Abdel) Rafi, which meant servant of one of the ninety-nine divine attributes of God. Rafi translates as the Exalter. We all possess at one point or another divine attributes, such as Hakim (the Judge), Jamil (the Beautiful), Latif (the Subtle), Rahim (the Compassionate), that intersect within us and without us and manifest themselves when we practice our mindfulness through the various forms of worship and practices offered by the Sufi Path.

I quit drinking alcohol, learned my Arabic prayers from a small booklet I found at a used bookstore and started praying five times a day. I remember the first time I rolled out my prayer rug and sung the *Adhan*, the call to prayer, with a slight Dylanesque intonation, feeling the drops of water from the ablution still trickling down my face, tickling my nose and ears, and then the plunge, the bowing into the unknown, trying to rid myself of any negative thoughts. Just like in those early days of French school, I basically faked it till I made it.

The Sufi Order would gather twice a week. On Mondays for *meshk,* which started with live music and the singing of devotional songs in Turkish, followed by *sohbet*, a talk led by Sherif and Cem, his Turkish American interpreter, on the principles of Sufism, its cosmology, its living systems and its morality, all told through Socratic methods and mind-bending tales that swallowed themselves in spiraling motions. Sherif would cultivate contradictions in his overflowing garden of parables and offer them to us like sacred meat from a sacrifice. And then there was *zikr* on Thursday nights, the Ceremony of Divine Remembrance, a time to remember together and pray and dance in circles accompanied by loud drumming and chanting. Sometimes it was outdoors around a giant bonfire the size of an elephant, where dervishes would whirl with fire and we would get lost in the fumes and the primitive intensity of it all. The Sufi Order had deep Asian shamanistic influences and the electric buzz, the deep guttural breaths of Allah—the cries, the barks, the roars, the silence, the ecstasy, hand in hand, step by step . . . it was exhilarating. It was like being inside Rumi's poetry, intoxicated and sober at the same time while dancing on the edge of a roof. And there definitely was an edge to it. On this path, I was cutting myself wide open, allowing all my faults and mistakes to rise to the surface under the critical gaze of my own moral microscope. Every little fault, every little hypocritical way of being became worthy of a thousand lashes from my newly awakened consciousness.

I remember forcing myself to drive under the speed limit and slow down before the light turned red and restrain myself from tailgating and cutting corners and impatiently honking at other cars.

"You think you're aware of yourself?" Sherif would tell us. "Catch yourself while driving. See how you behave at the checkout counter, how much patience you have with your children, with your wife, how comfortable you are waiting in an uncomfortable chair, and then let's see how awake you are!"

I was getting a graduate degree in hyper-consciousness as I walked the path of unconditional love. Every day on this new path was a gentle reminder that I was a newly born father placed on Earth to deal with and heal the nail wounds I carried inside.

I remember late at night, during those first precious months of the new millennium, holding my new-born daughter Isabella in my arms and feeling the colic rippling through her body like a series of electric shocks. The pain seemed to turn itself on and off without rhyme or reason. She cried and cried, and I could feel the helplessness that must overcome every parent who watches their children suffer. I experienced the guilt, the feelings of inadequacy, the steps taken to cover up the pain by diluting it with food or a pacifier. Listening to her cries at the time, I couldn't get Elián Gonzales out of my mind. He was the famous six-year-old, shipwrecked Cuban boy whose mother had drowned while trying to escape to the USA with him and her brother. After the tragic loss of his mother, Elián found himself at the center of an international custody battle between his relatives in Miami, who wanted to keep him in the United States and his father, who wanted him returned to Cuba. There are no easy answers when we are forced to confront the many contradictions we experience as parents in a world that teaches us to be afraid of pain.

I look around, and it seems that everything is created and sold in order to make our lives more comfortable, in order to "shield us" from certain painful realities; such as death, divorce, loneliness, separation, children in cages ... As I watched the news, riveted by Elian's tragic story, I understood what Elian's Miami relatives were trying to do for him and for themselves. They believed in the promise of American democracy and that a quick trip to Disney World would help heal his trauma. Instead, they were applying make-up to cover an open scar, distorting what should have been the boy's private mourning process into a self-serving political circus of hatred against Castro and the Cuban Revolution. Although I disagreed with their politics, I felt sorry for the Miami relatives. I could see that they had not been able to come to terms with the pain of their exile and the loss of their country. They were desperately clinging to that little boy for an answer to their own unresolved psychological conflicts.

As a child of exile, I hoped that my daughter would not grow up wandering the world and that I would be able to give her what had been stolen from me when I was young: a homeland and the security of a stable existence. I saw her birth as a chance to break my family's painful cycle of separation and fragmentation. In order to avoid pain, we take this avoidance to dangerous extremes of self-centeredness. Our actions become symptomatic of a deep sickness in our hearts. When we deny our pain, we waste our energies building artificial bubbles of comfort that will one day suffocate us. Just like they would suffocate Elián, or my own daughter Isabella, for that matter, if I were foolish enough to believe that I could control the amount of pain life will inflict on her.

And those Parisian nails of exile so deeply driven into my being? I was told not to take them out. But to love them. Yes. I was being asked to even love Pinochet.

"You must love the scorpion," Sherif once told me. "Just don't put him in your pocket. And one day, if you're patient, your poison might even turn into the fragrance of a rose."

He had one of his mischievous smiles that always made his words so much more palatable than any other bitter lesson I had ever been given. In the Turkish lexicon of Islamic cosmology,

this "love" was called *ashk*. It was unconditional and all con-
suming. It was the glue that held the universe together; it was our
path to becoming "beautiful human beings," as Sherif would
never tire of repeating during his long talks. It was a path of service and a path of sacrifice.

Holding Isabella in my arms that night, these thoughts had
an unexpected calming effect on me. The temptation to get my
daughter a pacifier slowly subsided. I kept rocking her gently,
whispering words of love in her ear as she began to quiet down,
as she always did at some point in the middle of the night. Sometimes I would sing to her my favorite Turkish devotional Sufi
song mixed in with my own made-up Spanish lyrics. But that
night I said a prayer of sorts, a prayer that one day Elián would
have the chance to become a father. And when he holds his
screaming child and feels his heart about to break, I hope he will
have the strength to embrace her pain and, like me, begin to come
to terms with his once interrupted process of mourning.

During my prayers, I could also hear another voice inches
from my jugular vein, whispering to me, "The home of your
songs was never a geographical place, like Chile, but a state of
being that comes to you when you free yourself from your so-
cialized, imposed identities and love all things without labels,
without grudges, without judgement."

I was beginning to heal.

Once you start making changes on the inside, as Alcoholics
Anonymous confirms, the world responds with a certain degree
of grace on the outside. Catalina Saffia, my second daughter, was
born in 2003, the day after I took my final oral exam at the University of North Carolina School of Journalism. It was a profes-
sion my mother pressured and cajoled me into pursuing. My
multimedia thesis, *Gnawa Stories*, was one of the first of its kind
in this new world of online multimedia documentaries fueled by
the fast-paced growth of bandwitch capacity which now allowed
the streaming of video and audio files. Part journalism, part
ethnography, it was the product of two years of intense travels

through Morocco and the world of the Gnawa who had opened their doors to my spiritual quest and trusted me with their stories. I now had a stable family, a US citizenship that protected me from ever being deported by any US administration and the professional multimedia tools to sustain that mythical home I had been searching for all my life. And then by some magic, Sherif selected me to be the president of the Board of Directors of the Rifai Marufi Sufi Order of America, a 501(c)(3) on a mission to build the Universal Center of Light, a spiritual retreat center on a large property in rural Mebane, North Carolina, donated by one of the dervishes in the order.

I remember a long day of weeding and clearing the land, with other dervishes standing over the small cemetery that came with the property where the remains of an unborn child had been buried. I felt such peace, such tenderness. The Dorfmans did not have a family burial plot anywhere in the world. My grandmother Raissa's ashes had been thrown to the winds in a communal grave at the outskirts of Buenos Aires after the family forgot to pay the dues to maintain the cremation niche. My paternal grandparents' ashes are in an urn on my parents' mantel in Durham, North Carolina. My mother's side of the family was buried in a faraway cemetery in the small rural town of Santa María, in Chile. It's not how you live, some say, but how you die. But what about *where* your remains are placed? Looking down at a piece of earth where I hoped to be buried one day, I could finally see the rest of my whole life before me with a degree of certainty and clarity I had never experienced before. I was sure that the curse of exile had finally been broken. For the first time in my life, I had found a community and a true teacher I could love and respect.

And that turned out to be a recipe for disaster. Never point to the ground and say, as if you know more than the winds, that this was where you will be buried. Unless, of course, you're willing to risk losing it all.

NUEVO SOUTH
(North Carolina, 2001)

"The one who calls himself a Sufi is not a Sufi," Sherif once warned us with a clever smile. And of course, he did not explain what he meant.

Sufism, very much like Zen Buddhism, relied on Koans, paradoxical stories similar to the classic, "What's the sound of one hand clapping?" The answer is usually, "I don't know," which is a good beginning for those seeking any type of knowledge. It's not a coincidence that one of the most famous books to popularize Sufism during the spiritual seeking mania of the sixties was Idries Shah's *The Wisdom of the Idiots*. I was fascinated by a path that made a virtue of challenging our assumptions about the world while mocking intellectual pretense and false hierarchies.

It felt very punk. But unlike the punk movement, we were not supposed to wear our spirituality on our sleeves. At least that's how I interpreted Sherif's warning in those early years when I decided to play it safe and keep my spiritual affiliation a secret from the rest of the world. I thought people would not understand it. Even if after 9/11, Sufism was being (incorrectly) branded in the West as the "gentle" side of Islam and Rumi was the best-selling poet in United States, I just didn't feel like having to explain myself over and over again. It was better that way. I could savor the thrill of my secret identity during the day and then, like a masked avenger, transform myself at night into a secret Sufi agent. I would put my daughters to bed, kiss my wife goodnight, grab my frame drum, my leather whirling slippers, my red and black cap and travel to the East, back in time, to what felt like the glorious days of Baghdad or Constantinople l in the sixteenth century. My everyday life, of course, was not spent in the sixteenth century, but in a region commonly known as the American South, a place I had only known, as a child, through the lens of one of my mother's favorite films, *Gone with the Wind* or Clint Eastwood's directorial debut *The Outlaw Josey Wales*—and the TV Series *Roots*. To further complicate this sense of geographical and cultural dislocation from my local surroundings, the "South," for me, was actually "El Norte." Whenever anyone would ask me where I was from, sometimes, if I was feeling playful, I would answer with a soft fake "Southern" accent: "Oh, I'm from down South." They would look at me with a perplexed frown and try guessing a few different states, until they got to the Mexican border and then, with a crafty smile, I would say: "Oh, no, I'm from way down South." The key here was to elongate the word "way" with the longest drawl imaginable and then deliver the punchline: I'm actually from Chile, in South America. And that—(I would pause for effect) is waaaaaaaay down South. No one, of course, could have detected a deep underlying tone of sadness and longing behind my joke. After all, I had given up on looking southward and going back to Chile and making Latin America my home again. I had relegated my childhood songs to some dusty forgotten corner of my dilapidated castle, and my geographical identity probably would have remained in this ironic state of suspension, neither here nor there, if it weren't that fate struck again and brought Latin America back to me, literally crashing on my doorstep with the intensity of a slow-motion tidal wave.

Starting in the early 1990s, an unprecedented wave of millions of immigrants of Latin American origin started to arrive, and more surprisingly, settle in the American South, a region that, unlike Florida and Texas, had never before experienced a sudden and massive influx of Spanish-speaking migrants. This wave was

part of a global migratory phenomenon, accelerated by techno-
logical changes like the internet, the global mobility of financial
and infrastructural capital, the automation of labor and the rise
of agribusiness, which was also bringing immigrants from Asia
and Africa to this Black and White, American South that still had
no idea how, or even the lexicon, to understand these "brown"
people.

When I first arrived in North Carolina in the late 1980s, you
could probably fit all the Spanish-speaking immigrants living in
my hometown of Durham into a small high school gymnasium.
Most of them, at first, came from South America, from places
like Colombia, Venezuela and Peru. Like my family, armed with
professional degrees and more often than not with the privilege
of fair skin and the right paperwork, they came ready to quietly
melt into the newly emerging, mostly white suburban middle
class, driven by pharmaceutical research, institutions of higher
learning and the coming tech bubble of the 1990s. Of course,
there were plenty of brown-skinned seasonal Mexican farm-
workers picking sweet potatoes and tobacco leaf in the fields, but
they were thirty to sixty miles away from Durham, out of sight
and out of mind, living in the dirt and squalor of old repurposed
slave and sharecropper quarters.

It's important to acknowledge that the American South and
Latin America had been in conversation with each other, in one
way or the other, since the 1530's, when the Conquistador Her-
nando de Soto, along with eight hundred soldiers, landed in what
they called La Florida (present Southern East Coast of the United
States) in his failed attempt to settle and colonize the region in the
name of King Philip of Spain. The defeat of the Spanish Armada
in 1588, made it more difficult and costly to forcefully respond
to encroaching English settlements like Jamestown. Soon after
that, Spanish maps were replaced with English ones in 1763, the
Spanish Quarter in New Orleans became the French Quarter, and
in 1845, in a supreme act of cultural appropriation, La Florida
became Florida, the twenty-seventh state. For centuries, immi-

gration from Latin America to the American South was so negligible that it did not even register in any official US census. Many were students, for example, like Fernando Bolívar, the son of Simon Bolívar, the great Liberator of Latin America, sent by his father to study at the University of Virginia in 1827. He was part of an historical trend that, to this day, brings tens of thousands of Latin-Americans to study in the United States each year. These sons (and later daughters) of the Latin American upper classes come seeking specialized higher education in careers like engineering, medicine and computer science, and also to perfect their English and learn how to internalize what it feels like to be "white" in a strictly racialized Black and White society. Others came as military officers to the School of the Americas, located in Fort Benning, Georgia, to train in guerilla counter-insurgency methods and torture techniques. After graduating, they went back to their respective countries like Chile, Argentina and Panama where many became notorious human rights violators. Some Cuban exiles from the post-1959 Revolution diaspora arrived in Atlanta and Charlotte starting in the sixties, but they quickly assimilated and never even created the semblance of a Little Havana. But the majority were just migrant farm workers coming from the Southwest and Mexico looking for better pay, filling up the empty rows in the cotton fields of Alabama starting in the 1920's or the tobacco fields of North Carolina; empty rows left behind by the Great Migration of African Americans fleeing the horrors of Jim Crow. Decade after decade, they passed through, some with visas, some without, following the cycles of the seasonal crops on their way North to the blueberry fields of Maine and the Apple orchards of Upstate New York. These migrants were for the most part single men, many called *Norteños* because generation after generation they traveled North, back and forth across the Southern border, leaving very little behind but the dust on their shoes and a few dollars at the general stores and local bars that would have them. For centuries, they were just mere shadows passing through the night—until the early 1990s, when everything started to change.

In those days, North Carolina, no matter how modern and shiny it imagined itself to be, was still a mix of that "New South" created after reconstruction as a means to attract Northern capital and find a less racist way to continue exploiting the virtues of cheap labor and that tired Old South still haunted by the ghosts of Jim Crow and the insidious legacy of redlining.

In the 1990s, however, and this was a blessing. The South had not yet been gentrified to the scale it is today. Living was cheap, land was plentiful and it was a safe place to raise your children. Early on, many who migrated to North Carolina were economic refugees fleeing the ravages of NAFTA, recruited, south of the border, to come work for example in chicken processing plants in Siler City or as Christmas tree harvesters in Appalachia, and in the construction boom right after Hurricane Fran laid waste to the state in 1996. At first, it was as if they had landed on the moon. They encountered a desolate cultural landscape void of comforts like local Spanish-language media, grocery stores with "Hispanic" products, bilingual social workers, Latino institutions or a settled, Spanish-speaking receiving community with decades, if not centuries, of presence in that region. This was very different from the experience of migrants moving to Texas, Chicago or California who could settle in already existing "barrios," where they could see their culture reflected back all around them. But still, the beauty and the warmth of the rural South reminded them of home, and unlike generations before them, they were now being employed in year-round industries—and they decided to stay. They sent for their wives and their children, and then their first cousins came, and their second cousins and, before you know it, everyone started having children and the face of the South would never be the same again. It was your basic white supremacist nightmare. At the same time, because these newly arrived immigrants could only afford to live in poor African-American neighborhoods, their presence also generated considerable tensions with mostly African-American working-class communities who were feeling displaced and threatened by a new labor force willing to work harder and for less pay.

The Latino population, in North Carolina went from 75,000 in 1990 to almost 400,000 in 2000, and then to over a million in 2020. Like me, in many ways, they had come to renew the promise of an American Dream that seemed to be slipping away from our national consciousness. We—notice the way I slipped into "we"—started building communities, literally from the ground up, taking over abandoned store fronts and mini-malls in little towns whose residents had never seen or smelled a fresh *tortilla* or a *nopal* cactus in their entire lives. The closest experience most rural southerners had with Latino immigrants was seeing them pick tobacco in the ubiquitous fields, or when visiting the racist South of the Border theme park in adjacent South Carolina.

"There's an irony here," a Cuban-American Republican state senator from Georgia once told me while I was filming a series of short documentaries for *¡Nuevolution!*, the groundbreaking museum exhibit about Latinos in the New South. "When you stop to think about the core values that Latino immigrants bring to the table—family, tradition, hard work and religion—these are the very same traditional values that old conservative southerners complain are disappearing before their eyes."

It's an irony that was not lost on me as I was trying to make sense of my own slow, roundabout subterranean transformation from a hyphenated "Chilean-American" immigrant with a green card into a full-fledged, card-carrying member of the "Latino" persuasion who can earnestly say, "Y'all," and get away with it.

"Latino" sounded like the singular American motto *e pluribus unum*—out of many, one. Out of many Latin Americans, one Latino community. It just made perfect sense to me. The moment you crossed the border, you left some part of your nationalism back home and you entered into what my ever-practical wife referred to as the American salad (rather than melting pot), because it allows a unity of taste while maintaining the uniqueness of each individual flavor and ingredient. Our own unique Latino salad allowed us to create a sense of unity and power out of a fractured and oftentimes powerless community under constant attack by xenophobia and racism. The term also reflected the political necessity of coming together and letting go (at least momentarily) of our own old grudges and racist blind spots to overcome the immediate difficulties of what it meant to survive as an immigrant in the South—a monolingual South that was not built to receive us. Yes, it was an ideal, and it still remains a very powerful one. So, we fake it until we make it, all the while recognizing how the term "Latino" contains the history of the erasure of the Afro and Indigenous identities that also make up the American continent. This is an essential moral reminder for those of us with relative privilege within the Latino community as we continuously check ourselves and make sure that every possible immigrant voice is being heard.

These controversial issues of identity politics were being talked about in letters, newspapers, community circles both big and small, public and private, and were reflections of the growing pains of a community that came from a continent fractured by nationalism, class, religion and race. In the New South, it was a community being forced now to not only live together in apartment complexes but also share power in ways that would be unimaginable back home. Cecilia Barjas, a Bolivian supporter of Javiera Caballero, the first Latina councilwoman in the history of Durham recently playfully shared with me the nature of this historical moment not so long ago: only in Durham can you find a Bolivian endorsing a Chilean. She was alluding to the dispute harking back to 1879, when Chile invaded Bolivia and stole its access to the sea, making it a landlocked country. Her observation was more than just an inside joke, it was a brilliant way to advocate for the ideal of Latinos in a nascent Nuevo South fight, day after day, *paso a paso*, to come out of the shadows and tell their stories as a first step to claiming their political and human rights.

In an effort to reach out to this fast-emerging, Spanish-speaking population, back in 1999, I was invited to contribute to the opinion pages of *Nuestro Pueblo*, a bilingual publication of our local paper, the *Durham Herald-Sun*. The publication of *Nuestro Pueblo* was meant to make the growing Latino population more visible to the majority community of Anglos and African Americans. I was a self-employed writer and my-then wife was a children's librarian. Our meager salaries were barely enough to sustain us. We could not afford new furniture, and I would regularly shop at a local thrift store.

I remember once listening to a salesclerk, a middle-aged Anglo woman with a thick southern accent, gently butchering the Spanish language in her honest attempt to communicate with two non-English speaking, working-class Latinos who were waiting in the checkout line. In those days, no matter where I went, be it the supermarket, the DMV, the mall or a garage sale, I found myself constantly acting as a translator and even sometimes a mediator between my two cultures. Being bilingual carries with it a heavy responsibility. Sometimes it demands that you intervene and enter private worlds; other times it allows you stay on the margins and observe, so to speak, the complex meanderings of new cultural encounters in the making.

That day, my conscience pushed me to intervene. I stepped in between the salesclerk and the two Latinos, doing my best to translate into Spanish what the Anglo woman was trying to say. After carefully listening to her story, I turned to them.

"Apparently, there's a gringo that paid for your pants," I said pointing to one of the pair of pants folded over one of the man's arms. "He saw you standing in line, holding them, and wanted to give them to you as a gift. The salesclerk took the money assuming the gentleman was a friend of yours."

The two Latinos gave me a disconcerted look and shook their heads in disbelief. They had come alone and knew no one in the store, they assured me, in that quiet and unassuming tone so common to Central American indigenous cultures. I could tell that they were beginning to feel apprehensive, as if some dark cloud was about to descend on their heads and wash them into a *Migra* van. "Don't speak up and don't make waves," is one of the golden rules of the undocumented community. After a few more confusing exchanges, the store clerk finally figured out that the mysterious man did not know them at all. He had bought the pants as an anonymous act of charity.

Adding to the uneasiness of the situation, the other customers standing in line at the register behind us were now watching the scene with growing impatience. I paused for a moment to consider the weight of my words, hoping that they would not further embarrass the two Latinos. I took a deep breath and explained that it was a gift from a stranger. This time they shook their heads, not in confusion, but with that strong sense of dignity so central to the survival of Latin American indigenous cultures, and put the pants down on the register. With a slight trace of anger in their voices, they told me they couldn't accept it and walked out.

I was left with a bitter taste in my mouth. I tried to imagine the intentions of this anonymous giver whose initial deed of charity had turned into a perceived act of paternalism. How could it be, I asked myself, that a gift could sometimes do more harm than good? How could attempts to communicate turn into a reason to alienate? The situation, at first glance, seemed far removed from daily experience. After all, we rarely go around thrift stores giving anonymous gifts or for that matter receiving them. And yet, something in that moment resonated deeply. This man was giving without really knowing those he was trying to help. He was imagining them as he wished them to be, rather than taking the time to know them for who they really were. And the truth is that we all make this mistake in our lives: governments, corporations, NGO's and individuals. We hold on to our preconceptions, and in the process we're unable to open our arms and receive others different from ourselves. We don't give. We impose ourselves on the world, from a thrift store to Afghanistan, more often than not creating more harm than good.

If only we could listen to the voices of this new millennium.

I was walking my two black labs, Tina and Stella, down Broad Street not long after that thrift store incident, when I crossed paths with a small group of kids on their way home from school. Like any other pack of teenagers, they were loud and exuberant, eyeing each other with that mix of tenderness and ironic detachment so typical of youth. Yet, there was something atypically southern in their demeanor. Watching them there in the streets of my hometown, and listening to the strange yet familiar language they were speaking, I felt a strong sense of complicity. They were speaking Spanglish, a mixture of English and Spanish spoken not only by millions of Latinos across this nation but also by millions of Latin Americans who have been thrown into the digital age and haven't quite made up their minds if they want to "surfear" the web or "navegar" el web.

However popular, Spanglish was and still is viewed as highly controversial. For many traditional English and Spanish speakers it was seen as direct attack on the purity of their respective languages. Some saw it as yet another face of American cultural imperialism, while others deplored the influx of Spanish into the English language as the vanguard of an army that came to topple it as the de facto language of the United States of America.

How easy it is to forget that what makes the United States great is not the purity of its language or race. Quite the opposite. The beauty and the power of the English language is that it is highly flexible. It has the potential to absorb and also be absorbed by other cultures and adapt itself to a world in constant flux, a fact that also fans the flames of the *English Only* movement.

Understandably, these attitudes are based on very real fears. People are afraid of losing one of the most cherished aspects of their identities: their language. And so, the question becomes, "What is an American?" We can also ask, "What is a North Carolinian?" The answers have to be seen in the context of this country's long historical love/hate affair with immigrants and the cultural vibrancy they bring with them.

Those Latino students walking down the street showed a healthy disregard for the norms established by the Royal Academy of the Spanish Language in Spain and the United States' Modern Language Association, whose handbooks dictate the proper uses of grammar, style and pronunciation of these languages. The students were actually making anyone who cared to listen aware of the internal, sometimes hidden mechanisms that shape the creation of languages and nations.

As an immigrant child who learned how to speak for the first time while living in the United States in the late sixties, using such words as "tomaña" to express the word "tomorrow," (a mixture of the English word for it with the Spanish word "mañana,") I found what was happening around me in Durham exhilarating. We have the opportunity to learn about our future selves, I thought to myself, but only if we're able to open our eyes and ears and listen to those students walking down the street with the kind of generous attitude that made this country so incredibly rich. If I had learned anything from those early Sufi Latino days, it was to not go down the dark rabbit hole of "I know more than you do."

In those daytime meanderings through a newly emerging Nuevo South, I could feel the Wisdom of the Idiots reminding me that sometimes the answer to a question is to give it a good spin and then let it go.

Yes, I was a secret whirling dervish Latino coming of age in the Nuevo South.

KURBAN
(North Carolina, 2003)

I held my glowing palm out, turning it back and forth in wonder. The day was chilly, gray and iridescent, imbuing on nature the kind of light that leaves no shadows in its wake. It was a beautiful day for a sacrifice. And for photography.

On this path we were asked to open our third mystical eye and carefully look within. I was never good at meditation, so I made that third eye my camera and fell in love with the idea of documenting my Sufi and Latino communities from within. Ironically, at the beginning of that documentary experiment, I got caught between worlds once again. In order to document a living community, I had to be both "inside" and "outside" of it. I wanted to fully participate and at the same time I needed to step back in order to reflect on it. The constant shift in roles and positions was putting into question my very sense of belonging; it made me feel alien, like I was neither here nor there. *Ni chicha, ni limonada*, as we say in Chile.

Earlier that morning, before the sacrifice, when I confessed to one of my Sufi sisters my simmering anguish, she said to me, "One should become 'big enough' to have both feet firmly planted in both worlds. These two states, the inside and the outside, are not exclusionary. It's all one, right?"

At any other time in my life, if anyone had ever used the phrase "It's all one" to reassure my existential dilemmas, I would

157

have dismissed it as trite or laughed it off as some hippy-dippy nonsense you drivel when you're tripping on acid or hugging a tree, or both. It was a testament to how far I had traveled down my spiritual path, how deeply I had rewired my brain, that her words had a profound impact on me. Through the teachings of Sufism, I had found the perfect opportunity to explore all the contradictions inherent in the power dynamics of documentary representation: I set out to document my Sufi order and the nascent Latino population in the South all around me. After all, at the center of the ancient Sufi teachings there was a profound moral, poetic, political and aesthetic tension, a tension that rises to the surface of everything around you when you begin to question the binary nature of the unconscious choices you have been making your whole life. I wanted to live on that fluid line, that sharp edge of the razor, that tightrope—pick your metaphor—between the sacred and the profane, between objectivity and subjectivity, between the eye and the eyepiece, between pressing "record" and pressing "stop," between the necessary critical distance needed to make aesthetic choices and the demands of moral engagement. I didn't want to experience the object of my gaze but the space between my camera and the subject of my gaze. I wanted my camera to become a truth-telling machine that contributes to the liberation of the undocumented father, mother, son and daughter into becoming protagonists of their own lives. I wanted to transcend, and I thought my camera would give me that power, however foolish and naïve that sounds.

That morning, I was at Fox Fire Farm, on the outskirts of Chapel Hill, a small town not far from Durham, ready to participate and photograph Kurban Bayram, known in Arabic as Eid al-Adha, the Muslim celebration, commonly known in the Old Testament as "Abraham's Sacrifice." In the Judeo-Christian narrative, God, testing Abraham's faith, commands him to sacrifice his "only son," Isaac. But, for many Muslims, the hero of this foundational story is Ishmael, Abraham's first son, born out of his maid servant, Hagar, after his wife Sara was not able, at first, to give him a child. As the story goes, thirteen years later, miracle of miracles, and (God does have a way to weave a twisted tale of intrigue and family discord) Sarah gave birth to Isaac, thus sealing the Convenant that would cement the fate of the Jewish people as the chosen ones, and lead someday all the way to Jesus and the establishment of Christianity as a prominent world religion. A few years after Isaac was born, in order to avoid any confusion and strife as to who was the legitimate son and heir, Sara demands that Hagar and Isaac be exiled to the desert, where, one legend goes, Ishmael settles the city of Mecca, becomes the original ancestor of the "Arabs" and with the help of his father Abraham (who in this version choses to side with the exiled refugees) builds the Ka'ba, the giant black cube at the center of the Hajj pilgrimage, on the very same spot where presumably Adam and Eve prayed together for the first time after leaving Paradise. When Adam and Eve left Paradise, according to Islam—and this has always fascinated me—their idyllic stay in Paradise had always been understood as transitory, since their departure to "Earth," had already been prophesized by Allah from the beginning. This story, in stark contrast to the Judeo-Christian cosmology, turns their loss not into a punishment, but into the just reward for having submitted, repented and shown the necessary humility to ultimately and responsibly handle one of God's greatest gifts to humanity: the power of free will. And so, in the Islamic tradition, in contrast to the Judeo-Christian narrative, Abraham does not deceive young Isaac and tells him what God has asked of him, and in turn, Isaac, exercising his free will, willingly submits to participate in the sacrifice. For better or for worse, they witness and empower each other, still within, of course, the confines of their (patriarchal) faith. Practiced for more than a thousand years, Kurban Bayram allows the participants to purify themselves through the external form of an animal sacrifice and engage in a communal spirit of giving by offering most of the food from the sacrifice to those who need it the most. It's a time for deep reflection and thankfulness. It's not an easy thing to witness, or to do for that matter.

There was a palpable energy in the air as a couple of dozen participants gathered around the hole that had just been freshly dug to receive the blood and later the offal of the ram about to be sacrificed. Somebody joked that we were going to run out of spots to dig. All around us in the ground beneath our feet lay the traces of past *kurbans* now part of the very same earth we were digging. We were all waiting for Sherif and his translator Cem to pick a ram. The knives had been laid on the cutting board not far from the hole, and a red rope had been secured to later hoist the carcass for butchering. In the distance, a donkey brayed loudly and Sherif recited a prayer in response. It is said that when *Shaytan* (Satan) makes himself present, donkeys sound the alarm. (It works every time. Sherif prays and the donkey immediately stops.) It was another lighthearted moment. Sherif turned to the group, pleased with himself, and explained the story to those who did not know it. For an instant, the energy in the air flowed in a different direction, allowing the sacred and the profane to mix and whirl with the cold winter wind around us.

That day, there were quite a few young dervishes who had never seen a *kurban* before. Many of them were vegetarians, and I could sense their growing discomfort. I had witnessed five sacrifices so far. The first one was in Morocco, before the Gnawa Lila ceremony that changed the path of my life. My head had been covered, and I was not allowed to see it as they slit the black goat's throat. It would not be good for me, I had been told. I thought of this as I watched some of the younger participants standing there in silence. The taking of life, of any life, is a heavy burden to bear. The intensity makes it such that the line between the one who holds the knife and those who witness can slowly disappear. Still, the knives belonged to Cem. He had sacrificed more than twenty-five rams since the day Sherif told him that it was now his duty to perform the *kurban*. He had been a vegetarian for fourteen years before that, Cem had told me. This one was possibly his last *kurban*. The taking of life was becoming more and more difficult for him. He looked at me as if saying, "Maybe it's your turn." I had been thinking about it and was moving in that direction, readying myself to take on that responsibility for the Order. It was not a decision to be taken lightly. You had better check your intentions before picking up a knife and slicing the throat of any living being.

For now, I just wanted to photograph the *kurban*. I was aware of the limitations of images to express the essence of things photographed. It all comes down to a question of faith and the spiritual value we gift those images with. Still, as I stood waiting, camera in hand, I was keenly aware that it was Cem who was going to have to hold that knife and take that life. In moments like those, emotional lines could shift wildly. In order to get the right focus with my manual camera, I had to remain fairly composed and in control, just as Cem had to in order to properly sacrifice the animal. I was keenly aware that my camera did not make me less complicit in the sacrifice. On the contrary, if this was to be my third eye, then the camera and the knife were one and the same.

Suddenly, Sherif and Cem walked to the pen where the rams had been herded. I could see Cem slowly approaching the chosen ram, indistinguishable from the others to my untrained eyes. He held the animal gently against the fence and knelt down beside him. I could see him whispering something in the ram's ear as he literally embraced him for what seemed like a long minute. It was a tender, private moment full of grace and sadness.

Silence.

Cem emerged from the pen carrying the ram in his arms, possibly just as Abraham had carried his son, and made his way to the place for the sacrifice. I approached them and put my hand on the ram's head to ask his permission to take his photograph and thank him for his sacrifice. In Qur'anic tradition, since Ishmael willingly submitted to his fate, it's believed that the rams will do the same. It might sound presumptuous, or a way to divert our guilt to assume this, and yet, again, it is a question of faith. You either believe it or not. And you then assume responsibility for that belief.

Cem carefully set the ram down next to a bright, colorful yellow bucket filled with fresh water. He gave the ram water to drink and washed him while Sherif held a lit incense stick near his face. Sherif then lightly placed his forehead against the ram's head and kissed him, soothing him with all the love and respect given to those who are about to sacrifice themselves for others. Imagine if every single animal we ate was given the time and the opportunity to die with dignity and care? Our world might be a very different place.

Everyone fell silent. I took a few photographs, keenly aware of the sound of the clicks that came with them, moving slowly, trying to stay out of the way, trying to negotiate my emotions as the ram was moved in front of the hole in the ground and another dervish tied his feet together. Cem, holding his knife in one hand, carefully massaged with his fingers the jugular vein that he was about to cut. Sherif called for a prayer. I was sitting on my knees across the hole, a few feet away from Cem who, with his long flowing red hair and his black ceremonial coat, set against the mercurial sky, the same sky that had seen countless moments like these unfold, was beginning to take on this incredible mythic quality. The world closed in. I could hear behind me the sounds of someone quietly crying. The ram was now calm and serene, and the more serene he was, the more emotional the moment became. Cem's eyes were closed, his lips moved imperceptibly as if in prayer, while Sherif put his hand on his shoulders for support and then let go, moving a foot away.

The hand held the knife, the knife was set against the throat. My eyes began to cloud over with possible tears as I told myself that I would not photograph when it first cut the flesh. Cem seemed torn in that moment, like the rest of us. He turned to look up at the sky, with his eyes like deep tunnels traveling somewhere far, then he looked down and began to cut the ram's throat. As the knife moved upward and through, some of the younger dervishes gasped as if they'd been holding their breath for an eternity. The blood began to flow, red, thick and steaming.

"Allah, Allah, Allah, Allah, Allah," Sherif began to chant over and over.

"Allah," everyone repeated in an incantation similar to the one that opens a *zikr* prayer.

The blood continued to flow, the ram kicked a few times, the voices grew louder. I joined in the chanting while clicking my camera.

Sherif dipped his finger in the ram's blood and placed a dot on the center of each of our foreheads. I stood up and moved my hair away to receive this blessing, then stepped aside, took a deep breath and shot a photograph. Forehead upon forehead, face upon face, I could see the weight of the world and the light of the world take shape before my eyes. It was an incredible moment, as it held together the past, the present and the future in one sacrificial red dot.

After a few minutes, the ram gave out his last fading convulsion and his final breath. He was dragged to the side, near a tall wooden fence to be skinned and butchered. The head was severed and placed on the wooden fence like a trophy. Suddenly, the energy had gone from sacred to almost irreverent, with cigarettes, Turkish jokes and laughter flying about. The sacrifice was over, we were back in the world of the profane. I knelt down and blew my breath into a small incision in the ram's lower leg, slowly filling him with air, separating the skin from the meat, making the butchering easier. His leg was salty, earthy, tangy. I looked around at all my friends and companions, bathed in such comforting, soft light, and praised God for letting me be a witness to this community.

Sometimes we are given the opportunity, or we conjure it up ourselves—it's so hard to tell even now, to live in bliss or ignorance, or both.

Like most things in life, and as Adam and Eve were foretold, heaven never lasts.

THE FISH
(Turkey, 2007)

I had been on the road for the past two weeks traveling across Central Anatolia and filming various characters featured in my never released documentary, *American Sufi*. At one point, we had gathered in Konya, Turkey, for Rumi's 800ᵗʰ birthday celebration. Konya was made famous by the great thirteenth century Sufi mystic and best-selling poet Jelaludin Rumi, who was once asked why he chose to live in such a close-minded conservative city. He replied, in his own unmistakable way, that you can only find true comfort in Hell.

This somber and fairly conservative city was overrun with tourists from all over the world. It felt at times like a miniature Sufi Disneyland, where Mickey Mouse had been replaced by a whirling dervish printed on every souvenir imaginable. The mausoleum where Rumi is buried sits at the center of the Mevlana Museum, once the home of the Mevlevi Order, commonly known as the Whirling Dervishes. I had been to dozens of Sufi shrines in Morocco, Northern India and Turkey, and this one appeared, unfortunately, to be the least intimate of them all. After waiting in line for more than an hour, we were herded like sheep in front of the shrine, surrounded by a mixed crowd of devotees exuding their love with genuine tears flowing from their eyes and curious tourists stealing away a photograph or two, even though it was forbidden to take any. No candles, no praying, no singing and

165

certainly no whirling allowed. I remember once being in the middle of a *zikr* in a small tea house that served as our place of worship back in North Carolina, dancing hand in hand with other dervishes and feeling this powerful electric energy surging through me as we went round and round in a circle. I remember being suddenly aware of this feeling, and this awareness made me lose it immediately.

"Just like that," I told Sherif, "it was gone. Did my thoughts interrupt the flow?"

He smiled. "You can't interrupt the flow of Divine Love. No one can. You stopped feeling it because you separated yourself from the experience with your thoughts. It's always there and it will always be there. Next time, stay in your heart."

Back in the shrine of Rumi, looking around at my dervish traveling companions lost in adoring contemplation, I was trying to stay in my heart, but the space felt dead, dead as Rumi's corpse rotting in the ground, dead in my mind as that museum or the state-sanctioned whirling ceremonies and other exotic tourist attractions showcasing "Turkish folk culture." Sufism had been officially banned in Turkey in 1925 by Ataturk, the founding father of the Turkish state. He not only abolished all Sufi orders but also expropriated all of their assets. Since then, Sufi orders have had to survive as historical and cultural organizations, holding their *zikrs* in relative secrecy while doing their best to stay out of the political spotlight.

We joked that we were secret Sufi agents, and this added a playful layer of danger and excitement that, in retrospect, I'm quite ashamed of, since it was the product of the kind of privilege I detest the most. Maybe at the time I was subconsciously hearing the distant bells of cognitive dissonance, because I was definitively growing wary of this constant state of exceptionalism which came into contradiction with the foundational unitarian ideology of Sufism. We were all one with humanity and yet at the same time we seemed to think of ourselves as special and different (and perhaps superior?) because we belonged to this secret hidden path where, in the words of Matthew, many are called but few are chosen.

I had already started noticing small patterns of disturbing behavior that we excused because it was our teacher's behavior. Sherif would break the rules, here and there, in order to test us, it was explained to me. We were supposed to follow the example of the sheikh, and at the same time understand that since he was acting from a higher spiritual plane, imitating his actions could be dangerous for us. It was a classic process of rationalization: you test your faith by walking all the way up to the line and peeking over into the forbidden abyss, just enough to justify dipping your toes into it to challenge your desire for purity and perfection. I would observe this dance of the ego and let it go down the river of oblivion because, who was I to judge? After all, if politics was the art of the possible, then Sufism was the art of the impossible. At its center, resting beside Divine Love was the idea of *Sabr*, meaning "persistence" or "patience," which coupled with *Shukr*, thankfulness, was the foundation of faith. But I felt like I was running out of it.

A week later, we were strolling across the ancient Galata bridge spanning the Golden Horn peninsula of Istanbul on a glorious sunny afternoon in late December.

"Rafi, we are just like that fish," Sherif said to me, pointing to a bloody bucket next to an old wrinkled fisherman. With the sun in his eyes and an unfiltered cigarette dangling from his lips, the fisherman seemed unaware of us.

Sherif stopped and turned to me. "We only open our mouths and eyes, gasping for the truth, when it's too late," he said, with a twinkle in his eyes. Sherif would sometimes use a metaphysical two-by-four to remind us that we should not waste our precious time on this Earth living deaf, dumb and blind to the divine love that is our ether.

I took my camera and began to film the fish flailing in the bucket, his desperate bulging eyes staring at me through the lens as if saying, "So, this is it? I'm dying and all that will be left of me is some video used to illustrate the foolishness of human existence?"

I felt a slight nausea. On my last night in Istanbul, the night of the holiday of Kurban Bayram, five years after I had photographed it back in North Carolina with such hopes for a small quiet place in the world, I had a dream. That dream would lead, with the precise mechanism of a cosmic clock, to the end of my Sufi paradise.

THE DREAM
(Turkey, 2007)

On my last night in Turkey, I had slept on a small cot in a hotel in Istanbul. That night, I dreamt I was back in North Carolina and the Sufi Order had gathered in a large meeting room for the Feast of the Sacrifice. Sherif handed me a large wooden spoon, almost the size of my head, and pointed to an enormous steaming cauldron of sacrificial stew meat. He gestured for me to serve the meal.

I obeyed, as a good disciple should, stepped to the cauldron of food and advised all the dervishes to line up for dinner. They looked hungry and rowdy, and before I could even start, they all began to complain that I was not doing it right. They pushed and elbowed each other to get to the front of the line. Before I could stop them, they grabbed their bowls and started scooping up the food themselves like a pack of ravenous wolves.

I stepped back and observed the scene in shock. All the dervishes had turned into their *nafs*, or animal selves. The evolutionary spiritual ladder in Sufism is best understood as an upward spiraling movement through the different levels of the self. Dervishes start on the first level, the one dominated by our lower animal self, the one that gives us free rein to be selfish, brutal and individualistic. It works wonders for a lot of people, and sometimes it feels like we organize our societies to feed our selfish animals. Then, through some life changing event that opens

169

our hearts to the world, we realize that selfish actions have consequences; this epiphany leads to the second level, which is usually transitory. That's when we realize how carelessness hurts others, especially the ones we love, so we decide to change our ways and begin to slowly domesticate those wild animals moving without a care through the world. Once we achieve control of our actions, we enter the third level. That is the level the vast majority of adult humanity is stuck in. It is where the universe clearly responds by rewarding us with positive, tangible changes in our lives when we exercise the art of mindfulness. We basically become wizards of our own existence, endowed with superpowers that give us the illusion that we can reach for a limitless sky. Sherif would often describe this level as a hell of mirrors, because people are never quite sure which image is the reflection of the ego or of the true self, the one to be trusted. Is it God? Is it the Devil? Life becomes more and more complicated, and we start hearing all sorts of voices telling us how best to live our lives. At this level, Sherif says, only a teacher can help us distinguish between our real selves and the ones trying to pull us back down into the dark pit of our selfish animal selves, just like I was being pulled down into the abyss of my dream of all those dervishes fighting each other to get a scoop of that sacred meat from the communal cauldron.

"Look at you!" I yelled at them. "Have you no manners?" I cursed them out. "Y'all are out of this Sufi order. Y'all don't deserve it. I'm kicking everybody out!"

And with those words, the dreamscape scene changed. I'm in my home. I march to my messy office closet and start looking for a very real big black binder containing all the establishing charter rules and regulations of the Rifai Marufi Order of America, so I can search for the exact legal passage, the precise wording, that will allow me to kick everybody out, once and for all.

I woke up before I could find the damn binder.

It was the morning of my last day in Turkey, and I felt sick to my stomach. I wanted to tell Sherif my dream before I went back to North Carolina and began the year 2008 with a renewed push to find the necessary funds to finish the Universal Center of Light. One of the ideas floating around the board of directors, I told Sherif as I knelt next to him in his small apartment on the Asian side of Istanbul, was to finally create a membership that would sustain not just the center itself, but also sustain him in his old age.

He nodded in appreciation and then asked me to tell him the dream.

After I finished, there was long pause.

"So, Rafi, you wanted to know, why did the dervishes in your dream not recognize your intentions? Why did they not trust you to serve the sacrificial meat?"

"Yes. I don't understand."

"Tell me, Rafi, did you do the sacrifice the way I told you to do before your trip to Turkey?"

"No. I'm sorry. I did not," I answered, lowering my gaze.

I was supposed to have taken the knife from Cem's hands and sacrificed a ram myself, but for some reason, or another, I never did.

"You were serving the meat as if you had made the sacrifice yourself. But you didn't. Your righteousness was a pretense, and the dervishes inside of you were just reminding you that you didn't deserve that responsibility. Go back to North Carolina and do the sacrifice. Then you can serve."

And I did what he ordered. And it was a sacrifice that no one expected.

THE SACRIFICE
(North Carolina, 2008)

One little mistake. That's all it took to set my world on fire.

I often wonder if any of this would have happened if I hadn't cc'd the whole Sufi Order listserv instead of sending a blind copy to their emails, as one is supposed to do. This slow motion train-wreck started when I sent out the first membership email at the beginning of the new year, 2008, inviting everyone to give their opinion on the future of the Order. I had carelessly exposed all 285 individual emails to anyone and everyone on that list ready to start a communal controversy with a long list of complaints. Or was this mistake just the accelerant for a fire that had been burning under the surface of the Sufi Order and would have risen to engulf us sooner or later?

After I sent the email, out of the blue, a new member from New York City who had recently moved to North Carolina while Sherif was in Turkey replied to *ALL* of the members on the list with a series of scathing comments, innuendos and veiled accusations of wrongdoing. It was what the Sufis call stirring the pot. And when you stir a pot, you never know what you're going to find at the bottom. And when some of us took a look, unfortunately, the bottom of our pot turned out to be burnt to a crisp. Everything happened so fast.

Unknown to me, email accusations of recent sexual abuse by a member in Florida had given a young woman in our order the strength to open up to her friends about past sexual abuse she had experienced as a child at the hands of one of the senior members of our Sufi Order. The abuse, it appeared, had been covered up for years. Then another young woman reached out with her story of abuse. In the blink of an eye, my beautiful Sufi Order had turned into a cult.

Our board met. After the women on the board spoke up and, to my surprise, shared stories of spiritual abuse at the hands of Sheri—after we cried, after we held each other tightly in that small office we used for our board meetings, the soft light filtering between us and the dust motes whirling around us, we fell into a deep silence. After all the emotions and attachments of the ego played themselves out, all I could hear were the words of my father in that diner long ago, almost ten years earlier, reminding me of who I was.

I was at the crossroads and, once again, I knew I was going to have to leave another life behind. I could literally see it in my mind, like a vanishing shore, a fading picture postcard fraying at the edges I had written to myself so many years ago in the hopes that I would never have to read it, never have to decipher its hidden message.

In that moment, I let go of the Teacher, the songs, the community I loved and the warm embrace of that piece of earth where I imagined one day my body would finally come to rest. I thought I had found a home, a resting place in the geography of the heart, but instead yet another exile was set in motion.

Three weeks after these revelations began to emerge, my heart pounding like a hammer, I opened the door to the closet in my home office and looked for that damned binder again. Yes, the one with all the rules and regulations I couldn't find at the end of my dream on the night of Kurban Bayram back in Istanbul. There I was, bucket-of-ice-cold-water-in-the-face awake. I grabbed the binder in my arms and closed my eyes, hoping that I would wake up from the nightmare and that everything would be all right again.

I reluctantly opened the binder to the page describing under what circumstances the board had the authority to expel Sherif from the Board of Directors, give away all the assets of the Order, including the land and the Center of Light, and then dissolve it. It was time to go to our lawyer's office and put an end to this dream-turned-nightmare once and for all.

THE MATCH
(North Carolina, 2008)

After being confronted with accusations of abuse in a hearing in front of our lawyers, Sherif immediately booked a flight to Turkey and left the country. His translator soon followed. In the end, legal charges were never brought, but, over the next ten months, more women came forward with accusations of spiritual abuse and we were able to partner with a local organization that offered resources and the support of trained counselors. The Order was financially dissolved and the Board donated the land and the half-finished Universal Center of Light building to the local Zen Center. Sherif never returned to North Carolina to teach again.

As the dust settled and the angry voices of those who refused to believe the allegations finally died down, I was left with an impossible question: If my spiritual teachings were based on a lie, then what would I do with all the lessons I had learned? If the root was rotten, it would follow that so were the fruits. My first impulse was to burn it all in a dramatic gesture worthy of the loss I had experienced. I was going to make it a moment to remember, just like those marbles in Amsterdam. And so, I filled a cardboard box with all my videotapes, hundreds of them, along with dozens of audio CDs and DVDs of every draft of my documentary *American Sufi*, thousands of negatives and photographs, newsletters and posters and song books. I even tossed in that binder with its rules for an organization that no longer existed.

I was so angry, so distraught. I didn't need any angels trailing behind me to pick up the pieces of my broken heart or some other Hallmark card metaphor to uplift my spirit. Nobody was going to put Humpty Dumpty together again. I just wanted to burn it all.

I lit the match.

HOME
(North Carolina, 2008)

Had I not learned anything? How many times can we glue back the shattered pieces of our lives before we accept that we are indeed broken beyond repair? My wife Primm asked me not long ago if I had any regrets. . . . You know, the big ones, the ones that will haunt you until the day you die.

I wish I could have answered yes, like everyone else. It would have made my journey less lonely, more comforting during the long winter nights. But, I can't. The truth is, I've spent most of my life taking the kinds of risks that should have killed me nine times over. I've made everyday impulsivity a virtue rather than a cautionary tale—*un tren sin frenos*, my mother calls it. When you're a runaway train, there's no time for regret, no time to burden yourself with the phantom limbs of past decisions good or bad. You light the match and you walk away, just like in the movies.

It's easy to forget, isn't it? To forget that we have been here before? As my father loves to say.

The tall match was burning bright. I looked around the yard one last time before setting fire to my memories. The apple tree we had planted for Isabella's birth was in full bloom; our resident cardinal who loved to perch on its branches was chirping, and the shed behind the tree needed a new coat of paint. There was weeding to be done in the vegetable garden, and we had forgotten to trim the azaleas.

Everything was its in place, everything as it should be. Except, not quite. I looked across the street and remembered that something was missing. How could I have forgotten so quickly? Where were the sounds of my neighbor's children playing in their front yard? Or the *ranchera* music blasting from the car stereo while my Mexican neighbor, Romero, changed the oil in his van and joked with his cousin about who knows what?

I had just returned a few days earlier from a short trip and found their rental house across the street empty and deserted. Did Romero lose his job? Did they have to move to a smaller home? Or did one of them get caught without papers? Maybe they just simply moved on.

Sometimes, I would smile and wave to them from the open window of my car on my way to work. Other times, I would walk by their house with little Catalina, say hello and exchange some pleasantries and gossip while standing on their tiny porch, taking refuge from North Carolina's scorching sun. They would often tell me how much they liked it here, the work, the weather, just like in Michoacán, Romero would sigh. He also loved the sense of community that brought the immigrants together. We would converse in Spanish about the Latino Community Credit Union and how best to get a car loan, the local soccer league and even basketball, and the best place to buy *nopales*. He'd reveal their hopes and dreams and sometimes nightmares. We were caught in the trappings of everyday life, *la vida cotidiana*, as we love to say. It was easy to forget that their mere presence here was nothing short of a miracle, a miracle that had literally turned my world upside down, even while I was whirling away with the Sufis at the end of the millennium.

My neighbor Romero was an integral part of this miracle, and now it was up to me to make sure his voice and his presence didn't simply disappear. Those of us who work and collaborate with mixed legal status communities have come to learn, by trial and error or sometimes by sheer instinct, that there is no need to ask someone like Romero about his nightmares or whether he is undocumented or not. Most of the time, if you know how to listen, the consequences of someone's status come up in casual conversation; a detail here, a comment there, a wink and a sigh. That's all it takes. And then, sometimes, when the relationship is deep enough, you can ask, "So, how was the crossing?"

It's taken me years since that fateful meeting in Santiago with the mothers of the disappeared to understand, as a documentary filmmaker, that creating the necessary space for someone to fully express themselves as a human being is the gold standard of our art and our craft. Of course, like everyone else, I'm curious, but I know that my curiosity is never reason enough to invite someone to open what could be a Pandora's box of emotions and longings. I trust that the other person also understands the healing power of telling one's story and appreciates having a willing audience listening, nodding, commenting, caring.

If you were watching us from afar back in those days, it would have looked like two men shooting the breeze by the side of the road, while shrieking children ran circles around them in delight.

Romero's story reminded me so much of my own past and how far I had come as an immigrant and how far others still have to come. I've always been the one leaving behind unfinished friends, vistas and gardens . . . . Now that I had settled down in Durham, I could finally enjoy what had been denied to me all those years: a view from a window that I could recognize day after day, for years to come; the shade of a tree I had planted, the ripe heirloom tomatoes that taste so much like Chile, plucked from a garden carefully, lovingly tended by my wife. If I didn't know where the hell I'd be buried, well, for now I could live with Isabella's tree, a soothing and reassuring thought.

And yet as I held that burning match between my fingers, I couldn't help but think that the stories of immigrants like Romero were now also part of my story. For years, I was the one who had left in the middle of the night; now I was the one who had to witness the passing of others. Happy stories of desert border crossings are far and few between, and Romero's was no exception. I had, on occasion, listened to his story, his eyes welling up a bit when he began to describe the scars left by giant thorns on his eldest daughter's arms, when they lost their path in the desert night.

"I call her my little tiger, *mi tigresita*. She likes that," he'd say with a smile.

It was a smile I had almost forgotten. It was the smile of a co-conspirator. With one look, he had made me an accomplice to his real secret: he was able to turn the violence and ugliness of the world into a tender, loving gesture for his daughter. It's the alchemy of a survivor's tale, the kind of gesture that brings you back from that pit of darkness into a place of safety and security. It's the tale that brings you back home, I thought.

Like so many of the tales still inside of you, whether positive or negative, whether you want to remember those experiences or not, they are still there, living, breathing you into existence. They are your experiences, and they have made you what you are.

Yes, I had learned something.

Every fire burns bright at first, the flames embracing each other like lovers rising upwards in a fast and furious dance, and you are captivated by the spectacle. You are mesmerized, Sherif would say. It is beautiful, but you cannot work or cook with those flames, cooking being one of the central Sufi metaphors to describe the spiritual development of the human being. The fire burns away, and then you're seemingly left with nothing but a pile of dead, godforsaken ashes. But if you look closely, if you care to bring your face to the smoldering ashes and you gently blow on them, you will discover that under them lies a burning coal hotter than any flame you've ever conjured up. And then you can start cooking. I had lost the Sufi flames and the forms that brought me to the fire, but I had been left with a precious realization: storytelling is belonging.

And in my life, filming is belonging.

I looked down. A soft breeze had blown out the match.

Thank you, I said.

It was time to get to work.

EPILOGUE
(North Carolina, 2018)

Dear Isabella,

I'm writing these words before you leave home for college

I wanted to give you one last gift, one last song that I have kept silent since your seventh birthday.

When people ask me where I'm from, I usually take a pause. And then I get lost in that pause. So where do you even start? How do you put everything back together again after it's been blown to bits? How do you erase all the borders of your life and in one pause find the answer?

So, where are you from? It's a simple question. You too will have to answer it one day, Isabella.

They say crossing borders is like being born again. And so, before you venture into the world, I want you to feel the collective blessings of your Latin American brothers and sisters who left behind their homes and loved ones, migrating by the millions to the southern United States, forever shifting and altering the course of its history. I want you to know that from Alaska to Chile, we are rejuvenating this country with our stories and with our struggle to make a home for ourselves in this new, emerging landscape. Our eyes, full of wonder, are blessed like yours, constantly reminding us of our own struggle to preserve, transform and share our new global southern identity; it is an identity linked to the ancient migrant traditions of colonization and assimilation, diversion and subversion. We have come to help transform worn old patterns with our slow and cautious embrace, the kind that begins when we cross the ballroom as we approach our future partner. And once we have looked into each other's eyes, the question then arises: Are we ready to come together on this bilingual dance floor of the New Millennium and dance through the night until the break of a new dawn?

For now, this much you can say: You are the first child in four generations of the Dorfman's history to reach the age of seven without being exiled from the country in which they were born. You and your sister Catalina broke our family's curse of exile, Isabella. And it means that no matter what happens in your life, no matter how far you travel, how many times you get lost in that sea of humanity we belong to, no matter what, you will always have a home to come back to.

If you need any other proof that you too are woven into the magical fabric of humanity and bound by the songs of love and resistance we sing to ourselves and to each other, then listen: Pinochet died the day after your seventh birthday.

Yes, it's true. Just like that. He just died.

That fateful day, before getting on the plane to fly back home from Chile, I went down to Plaza Italia to see the proof that our curse had been lifted with the death of a tyrant. As I stood there, tears flowing, one with my camera, one with the dancing crowds singing "*Adiós, General*," one with that resplendent *cordillera* of my childhood dreams, one with that guiding star beyond the sky always watching over me, I saw a small child through my viewfinder. He appeared to be all by himself, splashing in and out of water puddles, skipping and hopping between thousands of Chileans marching down the famous Alamedas you know so well, since I started taking you back to Chile. These are the same *alamedas* "that one day would open up," as Salvador Allende once told us in his last speech before he died, reassuring us that one day, we would all walk together toward a brighter future, like that child, untamed, free and full of wonder.

At that moment time seemed to vanish and I saw myself as a child of the revolution, before the coup, before exile, before the Pinochets of this world had entered my life.

And it was you, Isabella.

It was me.

It was us.

It was Paradise.

SELECTED FILMOGRAPHY

Angélica's Dreams (70:00)—2007

Angélica's Dreams, the first Latino feature to come out of North Carolina, is the moving story of Roberto and Angélica, an immigrant Latino couple torn between staying in the United States or returning back to their native country. When Angélica becomes pregnant, after years of being told that she was sterile, everything changes and the couple is faced with the difficult realization that one of them will have to sacrifice his or her dream for the other. Boldly mixing documentary and fiction, telenovela and comedy, director/producer Rodrigo Dorfman shot the film entirely on location in Durham, North Carolina, plunging his main characters deep into the daily life of one of the most vibrant new Latino communities in the country. *Angélica's Dreams* takes you into butcher shops, construction sites, churches, music festivals, bars and real estate offices. There are no guns here, no drug dealers, no gang members, no gratuitous violence or foul language, only the turbulent, unexpectedly humorous lives of everyday people struggling to enter the mainstream of American society. Originally conceived as an "educational video" commissioned by the Latino Credit Union, *Angélica's Dreams* is an attempt to go beyond the assumed limitations of the genre. It's an experiment that lies somewhere between the borders of fiction and reality, tragedy and farce, English and Spanish. *Angélica's Dreams* shines a refreshing new light for anyone interested in the possibility of creating low budget/high quality grassroots films from within a Latino community

Roberto's Dreams (97:00)—2009

After winning the Dora Maxwell Award for Community Service with its first feature film, *Angélica's Dreams* (2007), Latino Community Credit Union and local award-winning director/producer Rodrigo Dorfman produced the second part in this series of innovative educational hybrid feature films: *Roberto's Dreams* is a recession screw ball comedy that takes its storyline straight out of today's news headlines. In the midst of an economic crisis, Roberto has been laid off, Angelica continues to struggle with her house cleaning business and their ten year old daughter Brittany strives to mix her Latino roots with her American education. Roberto, like the Accidental Entrepreneurs featured in a recent New York Times article, decides to start the long and perilous journey of owning his own business: the first Latino green cleaning business in North Carolina.

Viva la Cooperativa (60:00)—2010

In 1999, a small group of community leaders came together to address the growing criminal violence against the North Carolina Latino immigrant community. Many Latinos, with no credit history and no prior experience with lending institutions, had nowhere to put their money. They were walking banks. The solution was the creation of the Latino Community Credit Union. This is the story of how a community came together to change their own destiny.

Generation Exile (70:00)—2010

When Rodrigo Dorfman was six years old, he was forced into exile because of the revolutionary activities of his father, Chilean writer Ariel Dorfman. Thirty-five years later, Rodrigo Dorfman weaves his experience of exile through the eyes of four women: a Taiwanese pianist haunted by nightmares of her past; an Afro-Caribbean Whirling Dervish on a pilgrimage to Turkey; a Latina artist mourning the destruction of her community and a young American woman caught in a web of spiritual abuse. Spanning four continents and a hundred years of personal history, Generation Exile is a meditation on our search for identity in a world full of pain and wonder.

One Night in Kernersville (20:00)—2011

Musician and bandleader John Brown is about to live the dream of his life: to make a big band Jazz recording. Set in the legendary recording studios of Mitch Easter, this short film takes you into the body and soul of what it means to be a Jazz musician today.

Tommy! The Dreams I Keep Inside Me (30:00)—2012

Tommy is a sixty-year-old autistic man with the lifelong dream of singing with a Big Band. Tommy, against all odds, armed with his golden voice and his all-American optimism, embarks on a quest to have the "world on a string."

Monsieur Contraste (61:00)—2013

Filmed during the tumultuous summer and fall of 2011, *Monsieur Contraste* follows the adventures of Jean-Christian Rostagni, a French photographer living in the American South who would rather stay true to the purity of his art than satisfy what he sees as the demons of marketing. When his wife gives him one year to make it as an artist or get a real job, he lands a gallery show that could be his last chance. *Monsieur Contraste* explores the work and the vision of a complex artist who has spent the last four decades making photography his religion. We see what it takes to create ambitious art, the process and its toll, physically and financially, on an entire family. The documentary was filmed on location in North Carolina, Washington DC and in New York City during the apex of the Occupy Movement.

Occupy the Imagination: Tales of Seduction of Resistance (90:00)—2014

Inspired by the uprisings of the Arab Spring, filmmaker Rodrigo Dorfman embarks on an exploration of his roots in 1970s Chile, where as a child he witnessed the first peaceful socialist revolution in history. Fascinated by the transformative power of art, Dorfman uncovers the power and legacy of his father's controversial book *How to Read Donald Duck*, which the military junta burned and banned for exposing Disney's hidden capitalist messages. When Occupy Wall Street explodes in New York City, Dorfman, camera in hand, begins a new quest: for the spirit of the Chilean Revolution in the euphoria of the Occupy Movement. A story of courage, defeat and resistance, this trans-American film examines whether revolutionary consciousness can awaken our imaginations in a world seduced and flattened by one ideology, capitalism.

And the Children Will Burn (13:00)—2017

Based on Ariel Dorfman's poem and story about two children who play "waiting for the enemy" under the shadow of a dictatorship, *And the Children Will Burn* translates this situation of terror to undocumented children hiding in a safe house somewhere in the New South. Migration, terror, machismo, hope and identity are some of the issues explored through the eyes of these children, who like so many, have to grow up too quickly in order to survive. Today, we unfortunately stepped from the metaphor into the real. *And the Children Will Burn* is an act of cultural resistance, a call to action that reminds us that if we do not stand up, our children will burn. Literally.

This Taco Truck Kills Fascists (61:00)—2018

New Orleans-based performance activist José Torres-Tama has a dream: to create a revolutionary Taco Truck Theater with a simple message: "No guacamole for immigrant haters." *This Taco Truck Kills Fascists* weaves two narratives: the classic "against all odds" story of an immigrant artist of color bringing the voices of radical black performers and undocumented workers out of the shadows, and the story of a father struggling to raise his two boys into political consciousness in the Age of Trump.

¡FIESTA! Quinceañera (54:00)—2018

Life for a Latinx immigrant family in the New South can be challenging and sometimes terrifying, but thankfully, there's always a *fiesta* to take you through the night. *¡FIESTA! Quinceañera* is a feature documentary based on the ITVS digital series that weaves the lives of three Latina girls and a seasoned drag artist as they celebrate their *quinceañera*, a complex and colorful rite of passage. The creative spirit of Latino communities and their struggle to retain their roots and traditions shine through this multicultural coming of age story for a new America.

The Shadow of your Absence (6:30)—2019

For the past two decades, Rodrigo Dorfman has been documenting the growing Latino immigrant population in North Carolina both as an artist and an activist. His work has taken him across the Nuevo South in search of stories of loss and hope, love and redemption. As an immigrant who has experienced the pains of exile, he has always been concerned with the separation of families by the border. One of the ways to engage was with the creation of "videograms" for migrant families divided by the Border. Before the age of smart phones and FB live, there were very few options for working class immigrants to visually communicate with the families they had left behind. The Shadow of your

Absence is one them. A videogram created from the dust and guts of the Mexican/US rodeo circuit, it's an experiment that deals with love lost, hope, machismo and frailty. It paints a collective portrait rather than focusing on one single individual, playing with the tension between the private and the public. It's a hybrid film because the immigrant experience is a hybrid condition, never quite here, never quite there, caught between fading memories and the sometimes-brutal immediacy of the now.

Quaranteened (54:00)—2022

Little Women meets the COVID generation as filmmaker Rodrigo Dorfman turns his lens inward in this intimate family coming-of-age story set against the backdrop of the first five months of the COVID-19 pandemic. *Quaranteened* follows the lives of four girls from a blended family in Durham, North Carolina, as they cope with the anxiety of their disrupted lives and stolen dreams with humor, self-reflection and just enough mayhem to pass the time as boredom sets in and the days begin to blur one into the other.

Bulls and Saints (52:00)—2023

After twenty years of living in the United States, an undocumented family decides to return home. Little do they know it will be the most difficult journey of their lives. Set between the backdrop of the rodeo rings of eastern North Carolina and the spellbinding Mexican hometown they long for, filmed over the span of seven years, *Bulls and Saints* is a story of yearning for home and reverse migration.

ACKNOWLEDGEMENTS AND THANKS

At first, I was going to share stories of both sides of my family tree, but as I started tracing my mother's side, I quickly realized how tortuous and convoluted this effort would have to be. For example, there's my great-great Italian grandfather who came as a doctor to the small village of Santa Maria, to treat the cholera pandemic spreading through Chile in 1870. Or my other great-great-grandfather, a German doctor at the court of King Otto in Greece, who barely escaped with his life in 1862 disguised as a woman after the King was deposed. He then pirated a shipload of spices, sailed to Peru where he made a fortune and married the daughter of a future president. And then there were more wars and fortunes lost, a series of family betrayals and bastard sons. The whole side of my mother's family tree feels like a James Michener novel on steroids or something straight out of *One Hundred Years of Solitude*. There's German, Croatian, Italian, Spanish and I am sure Moorish and Middle Eastern blood running through my mother's veins. I chose in my memoir to mainly deal with my father's Jewish family tree, because it's straightforward and more clearly stamped with the curse of exile, but I wanted to acknowledge my mother's side because, though her family story did not make it into the pages of my memoir, (my father partly tackled this saga in his book *Desert Memories* and I invite you to read it, if you are curious), I would not be the person I am without the stories of my mother's ancestors.

I want to thank my mother and my father for trusting and allowing me to be the person that I am. I also want to thank my first wife Melissa Chiti, for helping bring Isabella and Catalina into the world and allowing me, without questions, to chase my dreams wherever they might take me. And finally, I want to thank my wife Heather Primm and her family. Primm, as I call her, has stood steadfast by my side and has given me all the support a husband and a writer could wish for. She is the one who pushed me to see a doctor so that I could finally get diagnosed with the ADHD that has plagued my life. Without her, I would still be lost, trying to finish a book I had been struggling to write for more than 20 years. She has also given me a home where she grows tomatoes that taste just like the ones from my childhood in Chile. It's a small detail, but it makes all the difference in the world.